Modern Critical Interpretations

William Shakespeare's
As You Like It

Modern Critical Interpretations

These and other titles in preparation

Modern Critical Interpretations

William Shakespeare's
As You Like It

Edited and with an introduction by
Harold Bloom
Sterling Professor of the Humanities
Yale University

Chelsea House Publishers
NEW YORK ◊ PHILADELPHIA

© 1988 by Chelsea House Publishers, a division
of Main Line Book Co.

Introduction © 1988 by Harold Bloom

Printed and bound in the United States of America

10 9 8 7 6 5 4 3

∞ The paper used in this publication meets the minimum
requirements of the American National Standard for Permanence
of Paper for Printed Library Materials, Z39.48-1984.

Library of Congress Cataloging-in-Publication Data
William Shakespeare's As you like it / edited and with an introduction
   by Harold Bloom.
      p.   cm.—(Modern critical interpretations)
   Bibliography: p.
   Includes index.
   Summary: A collection of seven critical essays on the Shakespeare
comedy, arranged in chronological order of their original
publication.
   ISBN 0-87754-922-2
   1. Shakespeare, William, 1564–1616.   As you like it.
   [1. Shakespeare, William, 1564–1616.   As you like it.   2. English
   literature—History and criticism.]   I. Bloom, Harold.   II. Series.
PS2803.W55   1988
822.3'3—dc 19   87-15898
                                                                                      CIP
                                                                                      AC

Contents

Editor's Note

This book brings together a representative selection of the best modern critical interpretations of Shakespeare's comedy *As You Like It*. The critical essays are reprinted here in the chronological order of their original publication. I am grateful to John Rogers for his assistance in editing this volume.

My introduction meditates upon Rosalind's immense superiority to everyone else in her play. C. L. Barber begins the chronological sequence of criticism with his exegesis of Shakespeare's humorous recognition in *As You Like It* of the dramatic limits of representing "love's intensity as the release of a festive moment."

In Thomas McFarland's study of the play's complications, character interactions are seen as leading to an equivocal conclusion. Perspectives on pastoral are provided for us by Rosalie Colie, who presents the forest of Arden as "a countersociety, idyllic and playful, offering a model of possibility to the real world."

Existence in Arden is Ruth Nevo's subject, and informs her argument that Shakespeare attempted to replace Falstaff by the new combination of Rosalind and Touchstone. The play's social dimension is emphasized by Louis Adrian Montrose, who sees *As You Like It* as centered upon "intense and ambivalent personal bonds—between brothers and between lovers."

Sexual politics, one of our obsessive current concerns, is analyzed in its social aspects in the play by Peter Erickson. The same emphasis is taken up by this book's concluding essay, Barbara J. Bono's feminist reading of the play, in which *As You Like It*'s mixed genre is related to its plot of mixed or simulated gender.

Introduction

As You Like It is Rosalind's play as *Hamlet* is Hamlet's. That so many critics have linked her to Hamlet's more benign aspects is the highest of compliments, as though they sensed that in wit, intellect, and vision of herself she truly is Hamlet's equal. Orlando is a pleasant young man, but audiences never quite can be persuaded that he merits Rosalind's love, and their resistance has its wisdom. Among Shakespearean representations of women, we can place Rosalind in the company only of the Portia of act 5 of *The Merchant of Venice*, while reserving the tragic Sublime for Cleopatra. All of us, men and women, like Rosalind best. She alone joins Hamlet and Falstaff as absolute in wit, and of the three she alone knows balance and proportion in living and is capable of achieving harmony.

That harmony extends even to her presence in *As You Like It*, since she is too strong for the play. Touchstone and Jaques are poor wits compared to her, and Touchstone truly is more rancid even than Jaques. Neither is capable of this wise splendor, typical of Rosalind's glory:

> ROSALIND: No, faith, die by attorney. The poor world is
> almost six thousand years old, and in all this time there
> was not any man died in his own person, *videlicet*, in a
> love-cause. Troilus had his brains dash'd out with a
> Grecian club, yet he did what he could to die before,
> and he is one of the patterns of love. Leander, he
> would have liv'd many a fair year though Hero had
> turn'd nun, if it had not been for a hot midsummer
> night; for, good youth, he went but forth to wash him
> in the Hellespont, and being taken with the cramp was
> drown'd; and the foolish chroniclers of that age found

1

it was—Hero of Sestos. But these are all lies: men have
died from time to time, and worms have eaten them,
but not for love.

It seems a miracle that so much wit should be fused with such
benignity. Rosalind's good humor extends even to this poor world, so
aged, and to the amorous heroes she charmingly deromanticizes: the
wretched Trolius who is deprived even of his honorable end at the point
of the great Achilles's lance, and Marlowe's Leander, done in by a cramp
on a hot midsummer night. Cressida and Hero are absolved: "men have
died from time to time, and worms have eaten them, but not for love."
Heroic passion is dismissed, not because Rosalind does not love romance, but because she knows it must be a sentimental rather than a
naive mode. In the background to *As You Like It* is the uneasy presence
of Christopher Marlowe, stabbed to death six years before in a supposed
dispute over "a great reckoning in a little room," and oddly com-
memorated in a famous exchange between Touchstone and Audrey:

TOUCHSTONE: When a man's verses cannot be understood,
    nor a man's good wit seconded with the forward child,
    understanding, it strikes a man more dead than a great
    reckoning in a little room. Truly, I would the gods
    had made thee poetical.
AUDREY: I do not know what "poetical" is. Is it honest in
    deed and word? Is it a true thing?
TOUCHSTONE: No, truly; for the truest poetry is the most
    feigning, and lovers are given to poetry; and what they
    swear in poetry may be said as lovers they do feign.

Touchstone is sardonic enough to fit into Marlowe's cosmos, even
as Jaques at moments seems a parody of Ben Jonson's moralizings, yet
Rosalind is surely the least Marlovian being in Elizabethan drama.
That may be why Marlowe hovers in *As You Like It*, not only in the
allusions to his death but in an actual quotation from *Hero and Leander*,
when the deluded shepherdess Phebe declares her passion for the
disguised Rosalind:

Dead shepherd, now I find thy saw of might,
Who ever lov'd that lov'd not at first sight?

Marlowe, the dead shepherd, defines *As You Like It* by negation.
Rosalind's spirit cleanses us of false melancholies, rancid reductions,

corrupting idealisms, and universalized resentments. An actress capable
of the role of Rosalind will expose both Jaques and Touchstone as
sensibilities inadequate to the play's vision. Jaques is an eloquent rheto-
rician, in Ben Jonson's scalding vein, but Arden is not Jonson's realm;
while Touchstone must be the least likeable of Shakespeare's clowns. I
suspect that the dramatic point of both Jaques and Touchstone is how
unoriginal they are in contrast to Rosalind's verve and splendor, or
simply her extraordinary originality. She is the preamble to Hamlet's
newness, to the Shakespearean inauguration of an unprecedented kind
of representation of personality.

Richard III, Iago, and Edmund win their dark if finally self-
destructive triumphs because they have quicker minds and more power
over language than anyone else in their worlds. Rosalind and Hamlet
more audaciously manifest the power of mind over the universe of
sense than anyone they could ever encounter, but their quickness of
thought and language is dedicated to a different kind of contest, akin to
Falstaff's grosser agon with time and the state. It is not her will but her
joy and energy that Rosalind seeks to express, and Hamlet's tragedy is
that he cannot seek the same. Richard III, Iago, and Edmund superbly
deceive, but Rosalind and Hamlet expose pretensions and deceptions
merely by being as and what they are, superior of windows, more
numerous of doors. We could save Othello and Lear from catastrophe
by envisioning Iago and Edmund trying to function if Rosalind or
Hamlet were introduced into their plays. Shakespeare, for reasons I
cannot fathom, chose not to give us such true clashes of mighty
opposites. His most intelligent villains are never brought together on
one stage with his most intelligent heroes and heroines. The possible
exception is in the confrontation between Shylock and Portia in *The
Merchant of Venice*, but the manipulated clash of Jew against Christian
there gives Shylock no chance. Even Shakespeare's capacities would
have been extended if he had tried to show Richard III attempting to
gull Falstaff, Iago vainly practising upon Hamlet, or Edmund exercis-
ing his subtle rhetoric upon the formidably subtle Rosalind. Poor
Jaques is hopeless against her; when he avers "why, 'tis good to be sad
and say nothing," she replies: "why, then, 'tis good to be a post," and
she sweeps away his boasts of melancholy experience. And what we
remember best of Touchstone is Rosalind's judgment that, like a
medlar, he will be rotten ere he is ripe.

Perhaps Rosalind's finest remark, amid so much splendor, is her
reply when Celia chides her for interrupting. There are many ways to

interpret: "Do you not know I am a woman? When I think, I must speak. Sweet, say on." We can praise Rosalind for spontaneity, for sincerity, for wisdom, and those can be our interpretations; or we can be charmed by her slyness, which turns a male complaint against women into another sign of their superiority in expressionistic intensity. Rosalind is simply superior in everything whatsoever.

The Alliance of Seriousness and Levity in *As You Like It*

C. L. Barber

> *In a true piece of Wit all things must be*
> *Yet all things there agree.*
>> Cowley, quoted by T. S. Eliot
>> in "Andrew Marvell"

> *Then is there mirth in heaven*
> *When earthly things made even*
> *Atone together.*
>> *As You Like It*

Shakespeare's next venture in comedy after *The Merchant of Venice* was probably in the Henry IV plays, which were probably written in 1597–98. Thus the Falstaff comedy comes right in the middle of the period, from about 1594 to 1600 or 1601, when Shakespeare produced festive comedy. *Much Ado about Nothing, As You Like It,* and *Twelfth Night* were written at the close of the period, *Twelfth Night* perhaps after *Hamlet. The Merry Wives of Windsor,* where Shakespeare's creative powers were less fully engaged, was produced sometime between 1598 and 1602, and it is not impossible that *All's Well That Ends Well* and even perhaps *Measure for Measure* were produced around the turn of the century, despite that difference in tone that has led to their being grouped with *Hamlet* and *Troilus and Cressida.* I shall deal only with *As You Like It* and *Twelfth Night*; they are the two last festive plays, masterpieces that include and extend almost all the resources of the form whose development we have been following. What I would have

From *Shakespeare's Festive Comedy: A Study of Dramatic Form and Its Relation to Social Custom.* © 1959 by Princeton University Press.

to say about *Much Ado about Nothing* can largely be inferred from the discussion of the other festive plays. To consider the various other sorts of comedy which Shakespeare produced around the inception of the period when his main concern became tragedy would require another, different frame of reference.

As You Like It is very similar in the way it moves to *A Midsummer Night's Dream* and *Love's Labour's Lost*, despite the fact that its plot is taken over almost entirely from Lodge's *Rosalynde*. As I have suggested [previously], the reality we feel about the experience of love in the play, reality which is not in the pleasant little prose romance, comes from presenting what was sentimental extremity as impulsive extravagance and so leaving judgment free to mock what the heart embraces. The Forest of Arden, like the Wood outside Athens, is a region defined by an attitude of liberty from ordinary limitations, a festive place where the folly of romance can have its day. The first half of *As You Like It*, beginning with tyrant brother and tyrant Duke and moving out into the forest, is chiefly concerned with establishing this sense of freedom; the traditional contrast of court and country is developed in a way that is shaped by the contrast between everyday and holiday, as that antithesis has become part of Shakespeare's art and sensibility. Once we are securely in the golden world where the good Duke and "a many merry men . . . fleet the time carelessly," the pastoral motif as such drops into the background; Rosalind finds Orlando's verses in the second scene of act 3, and the rest of the play deals with love. This second movement is like a musical theme with imitative variations, developing much more tightly the sort of construction which played off Costard's and Armado's amorous affairs against those of the nobles in Navarre, and which set Bottom's imagination is juxtaposition with other shaping fantasies. The love affairs of Silvius and Phebe, Touchstone and Audrey, Orlando and Rosalind succeed one another in the easy-going sequence of scenes, while the dramatist deftly plays each off against the others.

THE LIBERTY OF ARDEN

The thing that asks for explanation about the Forest of Arden is how this version of pastoral can feel so free when the Duke and his company are so high-minded. Partly the feeling of freedom comes from release from the tension established in the first act at the jealous court:

> Now go we in content
> To liberty, and not to banishment.
>
> (1.3.139–40)

Several brief court scenes serve to keep this contrast alive. So does Orlando's entrance, sword in hand, to interrupt the Duke's gracious banquet by his threatening demand for food. Such behavior on his part is quite out of character (in Lodge he is most courteous); but his brandishing entrance gives Shakespeare occasion to resolve the attitude of struggle once again, this time by a lyric invocation of "what 'tis to pity and be pitied" (2.7.117).

But the liberty we enjoy in Arden, though it includes relief from anxiety in brotherliness confirmed "at good men's feasts," is somehow easier than brotherliness usually is. The easiness comes from a witty redefinition of the human situation which makes conflict seem for the moment superfluous. Early in the play, when Celia and Rosalind are talking of ways of being merry by devising sports, Celia's proposal is "Let us sit and mock the good housewife Fortune from her wheel" (1.2.34–35). The two go on with a "chase" of wit that goes "from Fortune's office to Nature's" (1.2.43), whirling the two goddesses through many variations; distinctions between them were running in Shakespeare's mind. In act 2, the witty poetry which establishes the greenwood mood of freedom repeatedly mocks Fortune from her wheel by an act of mind which goes from Fortune to Nature:

> A fool, a fool! I met a fool i' th' forest,
>
> . . . .
>
> Who laid him down and bask'd him in the sun
> And rail'd on Lady Fortune in good terms,
>
> . . . .
>
> 'Good morrow, fool,' quoth I. 'No, sir,' quoth he,
> 'Call me not fool till heaven hath sent me fortune.'
> And then he drew a dial from his poke,
> And looking on it with lack-lustre eye,
> Says very wisely, 'It is ten o'clock.
> Thus we may see.' quoth he, 'how the world wags.
> 'Tis but an hour ago since it was nine,
> And after one more hour 'twill be eleven;
> And so, from hour to hour, we ripe and ripe,
> And then, from hour to hour, we rot and rot;
> And thereby hangs a tale.'
>
> (2.7.12–28)

Why does Jaques, in his stylish way, say that his lungs "began to crow like chanticleer" to hear the fool "thus moral on the time," when the moral concludes in "rot and rot"? Why do we, who are not "melancholy," feel such large and free delight? Because the fool "finds," with wonderfully bland wit, that nothing whatever happens under the aegis of Fortune. ("Fortune reigns in gifts of the world," said Rosalind at 1.2.44.) The almost tautological inevitability of nine, ten, eleven, says that all we do is ripe and ripe and rot and rot. And so there is no reason not to bask in the sun and "lose and neglect the creeping hours of time" (2.7.112). As I observed [previously], Touchstone's "deep contemplative" moral makes the same statement as the spring song towards the close of the play: "How that a life was but a flower." When they draw the moral, the lover and his lass are only thinking of the "spring time" as they take "the present time" when "love is crowned with the prime." (The refrain mocks them a little for their obliviousness, by its tinkling "the only pretty ring time.") But Touchstone's festive gesture is *not* oblivious.

The extraordinary thing about the poised liberty of the second act is that the reduction of life to the natural and seasonal and physical works all the more convincingly as a festive release by including a recognition that the physical can be unpleasant. The good Duke, in his opening speech, can "translate the stubbornness of fortune" into a benefit: he does it by the witty shift which makes the "icy fang / And churlish chiding of the winter wind" into "counsellors / That feelingly persuade me what I am" (2.1.6–11). The two songs make the same gesture of welcoming physical pain in place of moral pain:

> Come hither, come hither, come hither!
> Here shall he see
> No enemy
> But winter and rough weather.
>
> (2.5.5–8)

They are patterned on holiday drinking songs, as we have seen [elsewhere] in considering the Christmas refrain "Heigh-ho, sing heigh-ho, unto the green holly," and they convey the free solidarity of a group who, since they relax in physical pleasures together, need not fear the fact that "Most friendship is feigning, most loving mere folly."

Jaques's speech on the seven ages of man, which comes at the end of act 2, just before "Blow, Blow, thou winter wind," is another version of the liberating talk about time; it expands Touchstone's

"And thereby hangs a tale." The simplification, "All the world's a stage," has such imaginative reach that we are as much astonished as amused, as with Touchstone's summary ripe and rot. But simplification it is, nevertheless; quotations (and recitations) often represent it as though it were dramatist Shakespeare's "philosophy," his last word, or one of them, about what life really comes to. To take it this way is sentimental, puts a part in place of the whole. For it only is *one* aspect of the truth that the roles we play in life are settled by the cycle of growth and decline. To face this part of the truth, to insist on it, brings the kind of relief that goes with accepting folly—indeed this speech is praise of folly, superbly generalized, praise of the folly of living in time (or is it festive abuse? the poise is such that relish and mockery are indistinguishable). Sentimental readings ignore the wit that keeps reducing social roles to caricatures and suggesting that meanings really are only physical relations beyond the control of mind or spirit:

> Then a soldier,
>
> . . . .
> Seeking the bubble reputation
> Even in the cannon's mouth. And then the justice,
> In fair round belly with good capon lin'd.
> (3.7.149–54)

Looking back at time and society in this way, we have a detachment and sense of mastery similar to that established by Titania and Oberon's outside view of "the human mortals" and their weather.

COUNTERSTATEMENTS

That Touchstone and Jaques should at moments turn and mock pastoral contentment is consistent with the way it is presented; their mockery makes explicit the partiality, the displacement of normal emphasis, which is implicit in the witty advocacy of it.

> If it do come to pass
> That any man turn ass,
> Leaving his wealth and ease
> A stubborn will to please.
> (2.5.52–55)

The folly of going to Arden has something about it of Christian humility, brotherliness and unworldliness ("Consider the lilies of the field . . ."), but one can also turn it upside down by "a Greek invocation to call fools into a circle" and find it stubbornness. Touchstone brings out another kind of latent irony about pastoral joys when he plays the role of a discontented exile from the court:

> CORIN: And how like you this shepherd's life, Master
> Touchstone?
> TOUCHSTONE: Truly, shepherd, in respect of itself, it is a
> good life; but in respect that it is a shepherd's life, it
> is naught. In respect that it is solitary, I like it very well;
> but in respect that it is private, it is a very vile life.
> Now in respect it is in the fields, it pleaseth me well;
> but in respect it is not in the court, it is tedious. As
> it is a spare life, look you, it fits my humour well; but
> as there is no more plenty in it, it goes much against
> my stomach.
>
> (3.2.12–22)

Under the apparent nonsense of his self-contradictions, Touchstone mocks the contradictory nature of the desires ideally resolved by pastoral life, to be at once at court and in the fields, to enjoy both the fat advantages of rank and the spare advantages of the mean and sure estate. The humor goes to the heart of the pastoral convention and shows how very clearly Shakespeare understood it.

The fact that he created both Jaques and Touchstone out of whole cloth, adding them to the story as it appears in Lodge's *Rosalynde*, is an index to what he did in dramatizing the prose romance. Lodge, though he has a light touch, treats the idyllic material at face value. He never makes fun of its assumptions, but stays safely within the convention, because he has no securely grounded attitude towards it, not being sure of its relation to reality. Shakespeare scarcely changes the story at all, but where in Lodge it is presented in the flat, he brings alive the dimension of its relation to life as a whole. The control of this dimension makes his version solid as well as delicate.

Although both Jaques and Touchstone are connected with the action well enough at the level of plot, their real position is generally mediate between the audience and something in the play, the same position Nashe assigns to the court fool, Will Summers, in *Summer's Last Will and Testament*. Once Jaques stands almost outside the play, when he responds to Orlando's romantic greeting: "Good day and happiness, dear Rosalind!" with "Nay then, God b'wi'you, and you talk in blank verse!" (4.1.31). Jaques's factitious melancholy, which critics have made too much of as a "psychology," serves primarily to set him at odds both with society and with Arden and so motivate contemplative mockery. Touchstone is put outside by his special status as a fool. As a fool, incapable, at least for professional purposes, of doing anything right, he is beyond the pale of normal achievements. In anything he tries to do he is comically disabled, as, for example, in falling in love. All he achieves is a burlesque of love. So he has none of the illusions of those who try to be ideal, and is in a position to make a business of being dryly objective. "Call me not fool till heaven hath sent me fortune." Heaven sends him Audrey instead, "an ill-favour'd thing, sir, but mine own" (5.4.60)—not a mistress to generate illusions. In *As You Like It* the court fool for the first time takes over the work of comic commentary and burlesque from the clown of the earlier plays; in Jaques's praise of Touchstone and the corrective virtues of fooling, Shakespeare can be heard crowing with delight at his discovery. The figure of the jester, with his recognized social role and rich traditional meaning, enabled the dramatist to embody in a character and his relations with other characters the comedy's purpose of maintaining objectivity.

The satirist presents life as it is and ridicules it because it is not ideal, as we would like it to be and as it should be. Shakespeare goes the other way about: he represents or evokes ideal life, and then makes fun of it because it does not square with life as it ordinarily is. If we look for social satire in *As You Like It*, all we find are a few set pieces about such stock figures as the traveller and the duelist. And these figures seem to be described rather to enjoy their extravagance than to rebuke their folly. Jaques, in response to a topical interest at the time when the play appeared, talks a good deal about satire, and proposes to "cleanse the foul body of th' infected world" (2.7.60) with the fool's medicine of ridicule. But neither Jaques, the amateur fool, nor Touchstone, the professional, ever really gets around to doing the satirist's work of ridiculing life as it is, "deeds, and language, such as men do use." [Ben Jonson, *Every Man in His Humour*]. After all, they are in Arden, not in Jonson's London: the infected body of the world is far away, out of range. What they make fun of instead is what they can find in Arden—pastoral innocence and romantic love, life as it might be, lived "in a holiday humour." Similar comic presentation of what is not ideal in man is characteristic of medieval fool humor, where the humorist, by his gift of long ears to the long-robed dignitaries, makes the point that, despite their pageant perfection, they are human too, that "stultorum numerus infinitus est." Such humor is very different from modern satire, for its basic affirmation is not man's possible perfection but his certain imperfection. It was a function of the pervasively formal and ideal cast of medieval culture, where what should be was more present to the mind than what is: the humorists' natural recourse was to burlesque the pageant of perfection, presenting it as a procession of fools, in crowns, mitres, caps, and gowns. Shakespeare's point of view was not medieval. But his clown and fool comedy is a response, a countermovement, to artistic idealization, as medieval burlesque was a response to the ingrained idealism of the culture.

"ALL NATURE IN LOVE MORTAL IN FOLLY"

I have quoted [previously] a riddling comment of Touchstone which moves from acknowledging mortality to accepting the folly of love:

> We that are true lovers run into strange capers; but as all is
> mortal in nature, so is all nature in love mortal in folly.
>
> (2.4.53–56)

The lovers who in the second half of the play present "nature in love" each exhibit a kind of folly. In each there is a different version of the incongruity between reality and the illusions (in poetry, the hyperboles) which love generates and by which it is expressed. The comic variations are centered around the seriously felt love of Rosalind and Orlando. The final effect is to enhance the reality of this love by making it independent of illusions, whose incongruity with life is recognized and laughed off. We can see this at closer range by examining each affair in turn.

All-suffering Silvius and his tyrannical little Phebe are a bit of Lodge's version taken over, outwardly intact, and set in a wholly new perspective. A "courting eglogue" between them, in the mode of Lodge, is exhibited almost as a formal spectacle, with Corin for presenter and Rosalind and Celia for audience. It is announced as

> a pageant truly play'd
> Between the pale complexion of true love
> And the red glow of scorn and proud disdain.
>
> (3.4.55–57)

What we then watch is played "truly"—according to the best current convention: Silvius, employing a familiar gambit, asks for pity; Phebe refuses to believe in love's invisible wound, with exactly the literal mindedness about hyperbole which the sonneteers imputed to their mistresses. In Lodge's version, the unqualified Petrarchan sentiments of the pair are presented as valid and admirable. Shakespeare lets us feel the charm of the form; but then he has Rosalind break up their pretty pageant. She reminds them that they are nature's creatures, and that love's purposes are contradicted by too absolute a cultivation of romantic liking or loathing: "I must tell you friendly in your ear, / Sell when you can! you are not for all markets" (3.5.59–60). Her exaggerated downrightness humorously underscores the exaggerations of conventional sentiment. And Shakespeare's treatment breaks down Phebe's stereotyped attitudes to a human reality: he lightly suggests an adolescent perversity underlying her resistance to love. The imagery she uses in disputing with Silvius is masterfully squeamish, at once preoccupied with touch and shrinking from it:

> 'Tis pretty, sure, and very probable
> That eyes, which are the frail'st and softest things,
> Who shut their coward gates on atomies,
> Should be call'd tyrants, butchers, murtherers!
>
> . . . .
>
>   lean but upon a rush,
> The cicatrice and capable impressure
> Thy palm some moment keeps; but now mine eyes,
> Which I have darted at thee, hurt thee not.
>
>   (3.5.11–25)

Rosalind, before whom this resistance melts, appears in her boy's disguise "like a ripe sister," and the qualities Phebe picks out to praise are feminine. She has, in effect, a girlish crush on the femininity which shows through Rosalind's disguise; the aberrant affection is happily got over when Rosalind reveals her identity and makes it manifest that Phebe has been loving a woman. "Nature to her bias drew in that" is the comment in *Twelfth Night* when Olivia is fortunately extricated from a similar mistaken affection.

Touchstone's affair with Audrey complements the spectacle of exaggerated sentiment by showing love reduced to its lowest common denominator, without any sentiment at all. The fool is detached, objective and resigned when the true-blue lover should be

> All made of passion, and all made of wishes,
> All adoration, duty, and observance.
>
> (5.2.101–2)

He explains to Jaques his reluctant reasons for getting married:

> JAQUES: Will you be married, motley?
> TOUCHSTONE: As the ox hath his bow, sir, the horse
> his curb, and the falcon her bells, so man hath his
> desires; and as pigeons bill, so wedlock would be
> nibbling.
>
> (3.3.79–83)

This reverses the relation between desire and its object, as experienced by the other lovers. They are first overwhelmed by the beauty of their mistresses, then impelled by that beauty to desire them. With Touchstone, matters go the other way about: he discovers that man has his troublesome desires, as the horse his curb; then he decides to cope with the situation by marrying Audrey:

> Come, sweet Audrey.
> We must be married, or we must live in bawdry.
>
> (3.3.98–99)

Like all the motives which Touchstone acknowledges, this priority of desire to attraction is degrading and humiliating. One of the hallmarks of chivalric and Petrarchan idealism is, of course, the high valuation of the lover's mistress, the assumption that his desire springs entirely from her beauty. This attitude of the poets has contributed to that progressively increasing respect for women so fruitful in modern culture. But to assume that only one girl will do is, after all, an extreme, an ideal attitude: the other half of the truth, which lies in wait to mock sublimity, is instinct—the need of a woman, even if she be an Audrey, because "as pigeons bill, so wedlock would be nibbling." As Touchstone put it on another occasion:

> If the cat will after kind,
> So be sure will Rosalinde.
>
> (3.2.109–10)

The result of including in Touchstone a representative of what in love is unromantic is not, however, to undercut the play's romance: on the contrary, the fool's cynicism, or one-sided realism, forestalls the cynicism with which the audience might greet a play where his sort of realism had been ignored. We have a sympathy for his downright point of view, not only in connection with love but also in his acknowledgment of the vain and self-gratifying desires excluded by pastoral humility; he embodies the part of ourselves which resists the play's reigning idealism. But he does not do so in a fashion to set himself up in opposition to the play. Romantic commentators construed him as "Hamlet in motely," a devastating critic. They forgot, characteristically, that he is ridiculous: he makes his attitudes preposterous when he values rank and comfort above humility, or follows biology rather than beauty. In laughing at him, we reject the tendency in ourselves which he for the moment represents. The net effect of the fool's part is thus to consolidate the hold of the serious themes by exorcising opposition. The final Shakespearean touch is to make the fool aware that in humiliating himself he is performing a public service. He goes through his part with an irony founded on the fact (and it is a fact) that he is only making manifest the folly which others, including the audience, hide from themselves.

Romantic participation in love and humorous detachment from its follies, the two polar attitudes which are balanced against each other in the action as a whole, meet and are reconciled in Rosalind's personality. Because she remains always aware of love's illusions while she herself is swept along by its deepest currents, she possesses as an attribute of character the power of combining wholehearted feeling and undistorted judgment which gives the play its value. She plays the mocking reveller's role which Berowne played in *Love's Labour's Lost*, with the advantage of disguise. Shakespeare exploits her disguise to permit her to furnish the humorous commentary on her own ardent love affair, thus keeping comic and serious actions going at the same time. In her pretended role of saucy shepherd youth, she can mock at romance and burlesque its gestures while playing the game of putting Orlando through his paces as a suitor, to "cure" him of love. But for the audience, her disguise is transparent, and through it they see the very ardor which she mocks. When, for example, she stages a gayly overdone takeoff of the conventional impatience of the lover, her own real impatience comes through the burlesque; yet the fact that she makes fun of exaggerations of the feeling conveys an awareness that it has limits, that there is a difference between romantic hyperbole and human nature:

ORLANDO: For these two hours, Rosalind, I will leave thee.
ROSALIND: Alas, dear love, I cannot lack thee two hours!
ORLANDO: I must attend the Duke at dinner. By two o'clock
    I will be with thee again.
ROSALIND: Ay, go your ways, go your ways! I knew what
    you would prove. My friends told me as much, and I
    thought no less. That flattering tongue of yours won
    me. 'Tis but one cast away, and so, come death! Two
    o'clock is your hour?

(4.1.181–90)

One effect of this indirect, humorous method of conveying feeling
is that Rosalind is not committed to the conventional language and
attitudes of love, loaded as these inevitably are with sentimentality.
Silvius and Phebe are her foils in this: they take their conventional language and their conventional feelings perfectly seriously, with nothing in
reserve. As a result they seem naïve and rather trivial. They are no more
than what they say, until Rosalind comes forward to realize their person-
alities for the audience by suggesting what they humanly are beneath
what they romantically think themselves. By contrast, the heroine in
expressing her own love conveys by her humorous tone a valuation of
her sentiments, and so realizes her own personality for herself, without
being indebted to another for the favor. She uses the convention where
Phebe, being unaware of its exaggerations, abuses it, and Silvius,
equally naïve about hyperbole, lets it abuse him. This control of tone is
one of the great contributions of Shakespeare's comedy to his dramatic
art as a whole. The discipline of comedy in controlling the humorous
potentialities of a remark enables the dramatist to express the relation
of a speaker to his lines, including the relation of naïveté. The focus of
attention is not on the outward action of saying something but on the
shifting, uncrystallized life which motivates what is said.

The particular feeling of headlong delight in Rosalind's encounters
with Orlando goes with the prose of these scenes, a medium which can
put imaginative effects of a very high order to the service of humor
and wit. The comic prose of this period is first developed to its full
range in Falstaff's part, and steals the show for Benedict and Beatrice in
Much Ado about Nothing. It combines the extravagant linguistic reach of
the early clowns' prose with the sophisticated wit which in the earlier
plays was usually cast, less flexibly, in verse. Highly patterned, it is
built up of balanced and serial clauses, with everything linked together

by alliteration and kicked along by puns. Yet it avoids a stilted, Euphuistic effect because regular patterns are set going only to be broken to underscore humor by asymmetry. The speaker can rock back and forth on antitheses, or climb "a pair of stairs" (5.2.42) to a climax, then slow down meaningly, or stop dead, and so punctuate a pithy reduction, bizarre exaggeration or broad allusion. T. S. Eliot has observed that we often forget that it was Shakespeare who wrote the greatest prose in the language. Some of it is in *As You Like It*. His control permits him to convey the constant shifting of attitude and point of view which expresses Rosalind's excitement and her poise. Such writing, like the brushwork and line of great painters, is in one sense everything. But the whole design supports each stroke, as each stroke supports the whole design.

The expression of Rosalind's attitude towards being in love, in the great scene of disguised wooing, fulfills the whole movement of the play. The climax comes when Rosalind is able, in the midst of her golden moment, to look beyond it and mock its illusions, including the master illusion that love is an ultimate and final experience, a matter of life and death. Ideally, love should be final, and Orlando is romantically convinced that his is so, that he would die if Rosalind refused him. But Rosalind humorously corrects him, from behind her page's disguise:

> Am I not your Rosalind?
> ORLANDO: I take some joy to say you are, because I would
> be talking of her.
> ROSALIND: Well, in her person, I say I will not have you.
> ORLANDO: Then, in mine own person, I die.
> ROSALIND: No, faith, die by attorney. The poor world is
> almost six thousand years old, and in all this time there
> was not any man died in his own person, videlicet, in a
> love cause. Troilus had his brains dash'd out with a
> Grecian club; yet he did what he could to die before, and
> he is one of the patterns of love. Leander, he would have
> liv'd many a fair year though Hero had turn'd nun, if it
> had not been for a hot midsummer night; for (good
> youth) he went but forth to wash him in the Hellespont,
> and being taken with the cramp, was drown'd; and the
> foolish chroniclers of that age found it was 'Hero of
> Sestos.' But these are all lies. Men have died from time
> to time, and worms have eaten them, but not for love.

> ORLANDO: I would not have my right Rosalind of this mind,
>   for I protest her frown might kill me.
> ROSALIND: By this hand, it will not kill a fly!
>
> (4.1.90–108)

A note almost of sadness comes through Rosalind's mockery towards the end. It is not sorrow that men die from time to time, but that they do not die for love, that love is not so final as romance would have it. For a moment we experience as pathos the tension between feeling and judgment which is behind all the laughter. The same pathos of objectivity is expressed by Chaucer in the sad smile of Pandarus as he contemplates the illusions of Troilus's love. But in *As You Like It* the mood is dominant only in the moment when the last resistance of feeling to judgment is being surmounted: the illusions thrown up by feeling are mastered by laughter and so love is reconciled with judgment. This resolution is complete by the close of the wooing scene. As Rosalind rides the crest of a wave of happy fulfillment (for Orlando's behavior to the pretended Rosalind has made it perfectly plain that he loves the real one) we find her describing with delight, almost in triumph, not the virtues of marriage, but its fallibility:

> Say "a day" without the "ever." No, no, Orlando! Men are April when they woo, December when they wed. Maids are May when they are maids, but the sky changes when they are wives.
>
> (4.1.146–50)

Ordinarily, these would be strange sentiments to proclaim with joy at such a time. But as Rosalind says them, they clinch the achievement of the humor's purpose. (The wry, retarding change from the expected cadence at "but the sky changes" is one of those brush strokes that fulfill the large design.) Love has been made independent of illusions without becoming any the less intense; it is therefore inoculated against life's unromantic and contradictions. To emphasize by humor the limitations of the experience has become a way of asserting its reality. The scenes which follow move rapidly and deftly to complete the consummation of the love affairs on the level of plot. The treatment becomes more and more frankly artificial, to end with a masque. But the lack of realism in presentation does not matter, because a much more important realism in our attitude towards the substance of romance has been achieved already by the action of the comedy.

In writing of Marvell and the metaphysical poets, T. S. Eliot spoke of an "alliance of levity and seriousness (by which the seriousness is intensified)." What he has said about the contribution of wit to this poetry is strikingly applicable to the function of Shakespeare's comedy in *As You Like It*: that wit conveys "a recognition, implicit in the expression of every experience, of other kinds of experience which are possible" [T. S. Eliot, *Selected Essays, 1917–1932*]. The likeness does not consist simply in the fact that the wit of certain of Shakespeare's characters at times is like the wit of the metaphysicals. The crucial similarity is in the way the humor functions in the play as a whole to implement a wider awareness, maintaining proportion where less disciplined and coherent art falsifies by presenting a part as though it were the whole. The dramatic form is very different from the lyric: Shakespeare does not have or need the sustained, inclusive poise of metaphysical poetry when, at its rare best, it fulfills Cowley's ideal:

> In a true piece of Wit all things must be
> Yet all things there agree.

The dramatist tends to show us one thing at a time, and to realize that one thing, in its moment, to the full; his characters go to extremes, comical as well as serious; and no character, not even a Rosalind, is in a position to see all around the play and so be completely poised, for if this were so the play would cease to be dramatic. Shakespeare, moreover, has an Elizabethan delight in extremes for their own sake, beyond the requirements of his form and sometimes damaging to it, an expansiveness which was subordinated later by the seventeenth century's conscious need for coherence. But his extremes, where his art is at its best, are balanced in the whole work. He uses his broad-stroked, wide-swung comedy for the same end that the seventeenth-century poets achieved by their wire-drawn wit. In Silvius and Phebe he exhibits the ridiculous (and perverse) possibilities of that exaggerated romanticism which the metaphysicals so often mocked in their serious love poems. In Touchstone he includes a representative of just those aspects of love which are not romantic, hypostatizing as a character what in direct lyric expression would be an irony:

> Love's not so pure and abstract as they use
> To say who have no mistress but their muse.

By Rosalind's mockery a sense of love's limitations is kept alive at the very moments when we most feel its power:

> But at my back I always hear
> Time's winged chariot hurrying near.

The fundamental common characteristic is that the humor is not directed at "some outside sentimentality or stupidity," but is an agency for achieving proportion of judgment and feeling about a seriously felt experience.

As You Like It seems to me the most perfect expression Shakespeare or anyone else achieved of a poise which was possible because a traditional way of living connected different kinds of experience to each other. The play articulates fully the feeling for the rhythms of life which we have seen supporting Nashe's strong but imperfect art in his seasonal pageant. Talboys Dimoke and his friends had a similar sense of times and places when they let holiday lead them to making merry with the Earl of Lincoln; by contrast, the Puritan and / or time-serving partisans of Lincoln could not or would not recognize that holiday gave a license and also set a limit. An inclusive poise such as Shakespeare exhibits in Rosalind was not, doubtless, easy to achieve in any age; no culture was ever so "organic" that it would do men's living for them. What Yeats called Unity of Being became more and more difficult as the Renaissance progressed; indeed, the increasing power to express conflict and order it in art. We have seen this from our special standpoint in the fact that the everyday-holiday antithesis was most fully expressed in art when the keeping of holidays was declining.

The humorous recognition, in *As You Like It* and other products of this tradition, of the limits of nature's moment, reflects not only the growing consciousness necessary to enjoy holiday attitudes with poise, but also the fact that in English Christian culture saturnalia was never fully enfranchised. Saturnalian customs existed along with the courtly tradition of romantic love and an ambient disillusion about nature stemming from Christianity. In dramatizing love's intensity as the release of a festive moment, Shakespeare keeps that part of the romantic tradition which makes love an experience of the whole personality, even though he ridicules the wishful absolutes of doctrinaire romantic love. He does not found his comedy on the sort of saturnalian simplification which equates love with sensual gratification. He includes spokesmen for this sort of release in reduction; but they are never given an unqualified predominance, though they contribute to the atmosphere of liberty within which the aristocratic lovers find love. It is the latter who hold the balance near the center. And what gives the predominance to figures like Berowne, Benedict and Beatrice, or Rosalind, is that they enter nature's whirl consciously, with humor that recognizes it as only part of life and places their own extravagance by moving back and forth between holiday and everyday perspectives. Aristophanes provides a revealing contrast here. His comedies present experience entirely polarized by saturnalia; there is little *within* the play to qualify that perspective. Instead, an irony attaches to the whole performance which went with the accepted place of comedy in the Dionysia. Because no such clear-cut role for saturnalia or saturnalian comedy existed within Shakespeare's culture, the play itself had to place that pole of life in relation to life as a whole. Shakespeare had the art to make this necessity into an opportunity for a fuller expression, a more inclusive consciousness.

For Other Than for Dancing Measures: The Complications of *As You Like It*

Thomas McFarland

To approach *As You Like It* immediately after *Love's Labour's Lost* and *A Midsummer Night's Dream* is to encounter a darkening of action and tone. The pastoral realm into which it enters has, in marked contrast to the moonlit forest outside Athens, genuine problems to ameliorate. The moment of pure pastoral celebration in Shakespeare's art is now forever gone. The motif of criminal action, which had been tentatively put forward in *The Two Gentlemen of Verona*, only to be banished from the golden confines of Navarre's park and Oberon's forest, now reasserts itself. *As You Like It* is a play that labors to keep its comic balance, and for this reason the comic reclamation in the Forest of Arden involves complicated character interactions and severe criticisms of behavior. The play exhibits more humor, but much less happiness, than its two great pastoral predecessors.

The situation at the start of *As You Like It* could, indeed, as well serve for a tragedy as for a comedy. The index to the state of moral well-being in Shakespeare's comedies is usually provided by the character and circumstances of the ruler. The mysterious illness of the King in *All's Well* casts that whole play into deviation from an ideal state; the lovesickness of Orsino at the beginning of *Twelfth Night* forebodes maladjustments throughout the Illyrian society. Conversely, the youth and magnanimity of Navarre, the puissance and benignity of Theseus, authenticate a pervasive well-being in their two realms. It is signifi-

From *Shakespeare's Pastoral Comedy*. © 1972 by the University of North Carolina Press.

cant, therefore, that the world of *As You Like It* is presented at the outset as a severely disfigured, for its ruler has been banished and his power usurped.

Grave though usurpation is, it is rendered still more grave by the fact that the usurper, as in *The Tempest*, is the brother of the true ruler, and the action of usurpation therefore reverberates with the archetypal crime of Cain. When Claudius faces his own offense, he says; "O my offence is rank, it smells to heaven; / It hath the primal eldest curse upon't, / A brother's murder" (*Hamlet*, 3.3.36–38). Neither in *As You Like It* nor in *The Tempest* does the crime of brother against brother proceed to murder; for such an outcome would put the actions of the two plays irrevocably beyond the power of comedy to heal. But usurpation and banishment represent the most serious kind of transgression. We recall the word that, in opening the somber action of *The White Devil*, casts all within that play into a nightmare of alienation: "Banished?" Or we recall Romeo's agony:

> They are free men, but I am banished.
> Hadst thou no poison mix'd, no sharp-ground knife,
> No sudden mean of death, though ne'er so mean,
> But "banished" to kill me?—"banished"?
> O friar, the damned use that word in hell;
> Howling attends it.
>
> (*Romeo and Juliet*, 3.3.42–48)

When, therefore, we learn that "the old Duke is banished by his younger brother the new Duke" (1.1.91–92), a mood of intense alienation settles over *As You Like It*. The mood is deepened by its foreshadowing in the relationship of Orlando and Oliver. "He lets me feed with his hinds, bars me the place of a brother," says Orlando (1.1.17–18). Indeed, it is bitter irony that in this play the comic motif of repetition doubles the Cain-and-Abel motif by extending it from Oliver and Orlando to the young Duke and the old Duke. In the supporting trope of Orlando and Oliver, moreover, the trouble between the brothers specifically involves, as does that of Cain and Abel, the relationship between father and son:

> My father charg'd you in his will to give me good education: you have train'd me like a peasant, obscuring and hiding from me all gentleman-like qualities. The spirit of my father grows strong in me, and I will no longer endure it.
>
> (1.1.60–65)

Their father being dead, the old servant Adam fills his place in the psychodramatic struggle, his name reinforcing the motif of "primal eldest curse." It can hardly be without significance that Shakespeare here slightly alters his source, for in Lodge's *Rosalynde* the retainer is called "*Adam Spencer, the olde servaunt of Sir John of Bordeaux*," and is almost always referred to by both given and surname. In changing "Adam Spencer" to simple "Adam" in the struggle of brother against brother, *As You Like It* conveys the sense of old woe ever renewed.

Beset from its beginning by such clouds of gloom and disharmony, the play must stake its claim to comic redemption very early. In the same conversation in which Oliver, fresh from his mistreatment of his brother and old Adam, learns from the wrestler Charles the "old news" of the old Duke's banishment (1.1.90), he, and the cosmos of the play, also learn of the existence of the land of pastoral wonder:

OLIVER: Where will the old Duke live?
CHARLES: They say he is already in the Forest of Arden. . . .
　　many young gentlemen flock to him every day, and
　　fleet the time carelessly, as they did in the golden world.
　　　　　　　　　　　　　　　　　　　　　　　　　　(1.1.104–9)

It is interesting that the play here invokes, instead of the Theocritan iconology of formal pastoral, the separate but intertwined tradition of the Golden Age; for the latter, by being more explicitly paradisal, more explicitly repels tragic possibility. Rapin urges in 1659, in his "Dissertatio de carmine pastorali," that pastoral poetry "is a product of the Golden Age." To Rapin, pastoral itself is "a perfect image of the state of Innocence, of that golden Age, that blessed time, when Sincerity and Innocence, Peace, Ease, and Plenty inhabited the Plains." So, to bring in the golden world so early, and entrust the message to such an unexpected source as Charles, is to go—not historically but semiotically—to the very fountainhead of the pastoral myth and thereby to concede the dire need for alleviation of the alienated mood.

Secure, then, in the promise of Arden's redemption, the play indulges in a still closer approach to tragic irrevocability. "I had as lief thou didst break his neck as his finger," says Oliver to Charles, perverting the latter's honorable intentions in the proposed wrestling match against Orlando (1.1.132). Oliver adorns the malignant proposal by language of studied villainy:

And thou wert best to 't; for if thou dost him any slight disgrace, or if he do not mightily grace himself on thee, he will practise against thee by poison, entrap thee by some treacherous device, and never leave thee till he hath ta'en thy life by some indirect means or other; for, I assure thee, and almost with tears I speak it, there is not one so young and so villainous this day living. I speak but brotherly of him; but should I anatomize him to thee as he is, I must blush and weep, and thou must look pale and wonder.

(1.1.132–40)

Such brotherly betrayal prefigures the relationship of Edmund and Edgar. And when Charles departs, Oliver's musing to himself suggests also the selfless dedication of Iago's hatred:

I hope I shall see an end of him; for my soul, yet I know not why, hates nothing more than he.

(1.1.144–46)

This play, then, involves the first massive assault of the forces of bitterness and alienation upon the pastoral vision of Shakespeare, and its action glances off the dark borders of tragedy. Indeed, the motif of repeated abandonment of the court, first by Orlando and Adam, then by Rosalind, Celia, and Touchstone, is prophetic of the departings and rejections of Cordelia, Kent, and Edgar at the beginning of *King Lear*'s quest for essential being.

It is, accordingly, both fitting and necessary that the second act of *As You Like It* opens with an equally massive attempt to restore comic benignity and to check the tragic tendency. For the rightful ruler, Duke Senior, without preliminary of action, invokes the pastoral vision and the idea of a new society in extraordinarily specific terms. In fact, the social assurance of comedy, the environmental assurance of pastoral, and the religious implication of both, are all established by the Duke's speech:

> Now, my co-mates and brothers in exile,
> Hath not old custom made this life more sweet
> Than that of painted pomp? Are not these woods
> More free from peril than the envious court?
> Here feel we not the penalty of Adam,
> The seasons' difference; as the icy fang
> And churlish chiding of the winter's wind,

Which when it bites and blows upon my body,
Even till I shrink with cold, I smile and say,
"This is no flattery; these are counsellors
That feelingly persuade me what I am."
Sweet are the uses of adversity;
Which, like the toad, ugly and venomous,
Wears yet a precious jewel in his head;
And this our life, exempt from public haunt,
Finds tongues in trees, books in the running brooks,
Sermons in stone, and good in everything.

(2.1.1–17)

But "good," despite the Duke's statement, is not "in everything" as it is in *Love's Labour's Lost* and *A Midsummer Night's Dream*; and the early promise of a "golden world" is not entirely fulfilled. The Forest of Arden, though a paradise, is not an unequivocal paradise; the "churlish chiding of the winter's wind," even if not painfully felt, is present. "Arden," as Helen Gardner notes in her well-known essay on *As You Like It*, "is not a place where the laws of nature are abrogated and roses are without their thorns." The gall of the court, before it is flushed away by the Arethusan waters, mingles and dissolves itself into the pastoral limpidity. Hence the existence of natural danger in the forest makes it a place halfway between reality and paradise. As Oliver says of his encounter with Orlando there:

A wretched ragged man, o'ergrown with hair,
Lay sleeping on his back. About his neck
A green and gilded snake had wreath'd itself,
Who with her head nimble in threats approach'd
The opening of his mouth; but suddenly,
Seeing Orlando, it unlink'd itself,
And with indented glides did slip away
Into a bush.

(4.3.105–12)

The presence of the serpent, potentially dangerous, indicates a certain admixture of harsh reality in this version of a golden world, for of that world Virgil stipulates that "occidet et serpens, et fallax herba veneni occidet"—both the serpent and the false poison plant shall die (*Eclogues*, 4.24–25). And in the Forest of Arden, an unpastoral danger is brought still closer by the lioness that almost kills Oliver:

A lioness, with udders all drawn dry,
Lay crouching, head on ground, with catlike watch,
When that the sleeping man should stir.

. . . .

This seen, Orlando did approach the man,
And found it was his brother, his elder brother.

. . . .

kindness, nobler ever than revenge,
And nature, stronger than his just occasion,
Made him give battle to the lioness,
Who quickly fell before him.

. . . .

In brief, he led me to the gentle Duke,
Who gave me fresh array and entertainment,
Committing me unto my brother's love;
Who led me instantly into his cave,
There stripp'd himself, and here upon his arm
The lioness had torn some flesh away,
Which all this while had bled.

(4.3.113–47)

The function of the serpent and the lioness are clearly revealed in these
lines: as figures of venom and fury, they symbolically accept the
burden of the venom and fury generated by the Cain and Abel contest
of Oliver and Orlando. The two brothers, their rage displaced into the
iconic beasts, are ready for reconciliation:

CELIA: Are you his brother?
ROSALIND: Was't you he rescu'd?
CELIA: Was't you that did so oft contrive to kill him?
OLIVER: 'Twas I; but 'tis not I. I do not shame
    To tell you what I was, since my conversion
    So sweetly tastes, being the thing I am. . . .
    When from the first to last, betwixt us two,
    Tears our recountments had most kindly bath'd,
    As how I came into that desert place—
    In brief, he led me to the gentle Duke.

(4.3.132–41)

Thus the Cain-against-Abel tragic disharmony gives way to the legendary
Roland-for-an-Oliver togetherness implied by the brothers' names.

The seriousness of the deviances to be reclaimed is to be found not only in a slight deterioration in the pastoral environment, but also in the introduction of Jaques, a pastorally untypical character. Jaques is a humor figure representing the type of the malcontent; he is a member of the tribe not only of Marston's Malevole but, in a sense, of Hamlet himself. Like Hamlet, he calls into question all aspects of life that fall below an exalted ideal of human conduct. It is significant that the first mention of his name refers to his awareness of this less-than-ideal pastoral environment. The old Duke says:

> Come, shall we go and kill us venison?
> And yet it irks me the poor dappled fools,
> Being native burghers of this desert city,
> Should, in their own confines, with forked heads
> Have their round haunches gor'd.
> FIRST LORD: Indeed, my lord,
> The melancholy Jaques grieves at that;
> And, in that kind, swears you do more usurp
> Than doth your brother that hath banish'd you.
>   (2.1.21–28)

It is emphasized that the Forest of Arden is a version of pastoral like Robin Hood's Sherwood Forest (Charles had said at the outset that "in the forest of Arden" the Duke and his retainers "live like the old Robin Hood of England" [1.1.105–9]). The specification not only prefigures Jonson's pastoral variant, whose "scene is Sherwood" (*The Sad Shepherd*, Prologue.), but it also indicates a world somewhat less perfect than Ovid's golden age. Indeed, as Elizabeth Armstrong points out, "Peace between man and the animal creation" was "a traditional feature of the Age of Gold"; and the "existence of this tradition" may have deterred Ronsard "from allowing his Age of Gold people to slay animals for food or sport" (*Ronsard and the Age of Gold*). The continuation of the First Lord's report suggests, in direct ratio to its length, the deficiencies of this only partly golden world:

> To-day my Lord of Amiens and myself
> Did steal behind him as he lay along
> Under an oak whose antique root peeps out
> Upon the brook that brawls along this wood!
> To the which place a poor sequest'red stag,
> That from the hunter's aim had ta'en a hurt,

> Did come to languish; and indeed, my lord,
> The wretched animal heav'd forth such groans
> That their discharge did stretch his leathern coat
> Almost to bursting; and the big round tears
> Cours'd one another down his innocent nose
> In piteous chase; and thus the hairy fool.
>
> .   .   .   .
>
> Stood on th' extremest verge of the swift brook,
> Augmenting it with tears.
> DUKE SENIOR: But what said Jaques?
> Did he not moralize this spectacle?
> FIRST LORD: O, yes, into a thousand similes.
>
> .   .   .   .
>
>   swearing that we
> Are mere usurpers, tyrants, and what's worse,
> To fright the animals and to kill them up
> In their assign'd and native dwelling-place.
> DUKE SENIOR: And did you leave him in this contemplation?
> SECOND LORD: We did, my lord, weeping and commenting
> Upon the sobbing deer.
>
>   (2.1.29–66)

The import of the passage can hardly be mistaken: the deer, with its human coordinates of feeling ("The wretched animal . . . the big round tears . . . his innocent nose . . ."), brings the reality of human pain into the forest; and Jaques's moral criticism, by linking the killing of the deer with usurpation and tyranny, indicates that the forest is not completely divorced from the reality of the urban spectacle. Jaques, indeed, links city, court, and pastoral forest together by his criticism.

Although a pastorally atypical figure in the play, Jaques is nevertheless in a sense its central figure, or at least the figure who does most to define the idiosyncratic strain of malaise. But the type of the malcontent can imply not only Hamlet's idealism but Bosola's cynicism, and Jaques's presence threatens as well as criticizes the pastoral environment. It is therefore necessary to provide him a counterweight, so that the unchecked burden of malcontentment may not become so heavy as to break up entirely the fragilities of the pastoral vision. That counterweight the play summons up in the character of Touchstone, the fool. Replacing the "hairy fool / Much marked of the melancholy Jaques" (that is, the deer whose travail brings out Jacques's role as in part the emissary of a realm of more beatific feeling), Touchstone reminds us, perhaps subliminally, of Jaques's compassion and at the same time dissolves the accompanying melancholy into a language of ridicule and jest more fitting to comic aims. The function of the fool is to redeem Jaques from the melancholy that is so dangerous to the comic-pastoral aspiration:

> DUKE SENIOR: What, you look merrily!
> JAQUES: A fool, a fool! I met a fool i' th' forest,
>   A motley fool. A miserable world!
>   As I do live by food, I met a fool,
>   Who laid him down and bask'd him in the sun,
>   And rail'd on Lady Fortune in good terms,
>   In good set terms—and yet a motley fool.
>   "Good morrow, fool," quoth I. "No, sir," quoth he,
>   "Call me not fool till heaven hath sent me fortune."
>   And then he drew a dial from his poke,
>   And, looking on it with lack-lustre eye,
>   Says very wisely, "It is ten o'clock;
>   Thus we may see," quoth he, "how the world wags;
>   'Tis but an hour ago since it was nine;
>   And after one hour more 'twill be eleven;
>   And so, from hour to hour, we ripe and ripe,
>   And then, from hour to hour, we rot and rot;
>   And thereby hangs a tale." When I did hear
>   The motley fool thus moral on the time,
>   My lungs began to crow like chanticleer,
>   That fools should be so deep contemplative;
>   And I did laugh sans intermission
>   An hour by his dial. O noble fool!
>   A worthy fool! Motley's the only wear.
>
> (2.7.11–34)

Thus, whilst Jaques criticizes the world, Touchstone gently and unintentionally mocks that criticism. Touchstone's own railing "on Lady Fortune in good set terms" reveals to Jaques the dimension of the absurd in all human seriousness. To hear a "motley fool thus moral on the time" is to suggest that to moral on the time is to be a motley fool. If a fool is "deep contemplative," then perhaps the "deep contemplative" is the foolish. Touchstone is a mirror that not only reflects, but lightens, the malcontentment of Jaques. Indeed, garbed in fool's motley, such criticisms as those of Jaques can safely be allowed in the pastoral realm. "Invest me in my motley," says Jaques:

> give me leave
> To speak my mind, and I will through and through
> Cleanse the foul body of th' infected world.
>
> (2.7.58–60)

But only if he accepts the dimension of the ludicrous as supplied by the fool can Jaques fit into the comic scheme:

> JAQUES: Yes, I have gain'd my experience.
> ROSALIND: And your experience makes you sad. I had
> rather have a fool to make me merry than experience to
> make me sad.
>
> (4.1.23–25)

Touchstone himself serves the same large function as his counterpart in *King Lear*, although his role is less wonderfully developed. The fool, in either comedy or tragedy, tends to criticize arrogance and pretense on the part of the other characters (he can make no claim to wisdom, but he is, notwithstanding, no less wise than the others). In comedy, moreover, his benign good nature provides an added depth of social criticism of the individual: the fool, who is isolated by his motley garb and supposed mental limitations, refuses to be alienated. Whereas Jaques, the malcontent, endlessly finds the world a woeful place, Touchstone accepts existence as he finds it. And most importantly, either here or in *King Lear*, the fool constantly urges the paradox of St. Paul: "If any man among you seemeth to be wise in this world, let him become a fool, that he may be wise" (1 Cor. 3:18).

Thus, as Jaques says, "The wise man's folly is anatomiz'd / Even by the squand'ring glances of the fool" (2.7.56–57). "The more pity," says Touchstone,

> that fools may not speak wisely what wise men do foolishly.
> CELIA: By my troth, thou sayest true; for since the little wit
> that fools have was silenced, the little foolery that wise
> men have makes a great show.
>
> (1.2.78–82)

And as Touchstone emphasizes, " 'The fool doth think he is wise, but the wise man knows himself to be a fool' " (5.1.29–30). By thus paradoxically collapsing the original juxtaposition of wisdom and folly into a playful equation where they are interchangeable, the fool reinforces those attitudes of Plotinus and Plato, mentioned [previously], by which we are urged to realize that human life, when all is done, is not a very serious matter.

This implication of the fool's influence is made explicit in the famous speech of Jaques, uttered after he has met Touchstone and expressed the desire "that I were a fool! / I am ambitious for a motley coat" (2.7.42–43); for the speech constitutes a change from Jaques's customary black melancholy:

> All the world's a stage,
> And all the men and women merely players;
> They have their exits and their entrances;
> And one man in his time plays many parts,
> His acts being seven ages. At first the infant,
> Mewling and puking in the nurse's arms,
> Then the whining school-boy, with his satchel
> And shining morning face, creeping like snail
> Unwillingly to school. And then the lover,
> Sighing like furnace, with a woeful ballad
> Made to his mistress' eyebrow. Then a soldier,
> Full of strange oaths, and bearded like the pard,
> Jealous in honour, sudden and quick in quarrel,
> Seeking the bubble reputation
> Even in the cannon's mouth. And then the justice,
> In fair round belly with good capon lin'd,
> With eyes severe and beard of formal cut,
> Full of wise saws and modern instances;
> And so he plays his part. The sixth age shifts
> Into the lean and slipper'd pantaloon,
> With spectacles on nose and pouch on side,
> His youthful hose, well sav'd, a world too wide
> For his shrunk shank; and his big manly voice,
> Turning again toward childish treble, pipes
> And whistles in his sound. Last scene of all,
> That ends this strange eventful history,
> Is second childishness and mere oblivion;
> Sans teeth, sans eyes, sans taste, sans every thing.
>   (2.7.139–66)

The lines achieve simultaneously a vision of life and a wry, rather than melancholy or despairing, perspective on its mystery. The tears of

Jaques's contemplation of the wounded stag, mingled with the merry wonder of Touchstone's motley, become now an equivocal smile. Jaques's attitude, accordingly, is reclaimed from tragedy; and as a mark of this reclamation it sees the vanity of human life in terms of social roles—schoolboy, lover, soldier, justice—rather than in terms of individual agonies.

Jaques's moralizing, however, is here, as in the instance of the sobbing deer, somewhat blunted by a certain misunderstanding of reality. In the earlier instance, he did not consider that the hunters were killing out of necessity and not for sport; now the generalities of his cynical seven ages speech do not relate to the actuality around him. For Adam, who by Jaques's speech should be in "second childishness and mere oblivion . . . sans every thing," is instead—and the point is made by Orlando just before Jaques begins to speak—an "old poor man, / Who after me hath many a weary step / Limp'd in pure love." Adam is not "sans every thing," but full of "pure love." Jaques's speech, in short, does not recognize the facts of human community and mutual concern, and flies in the face of the reality before him:

> ORLANDO: I almost die for food, and let me have it.
> DUKE SENIOR: Sit down and feed, and welcome to our
> table.
> ORLANDO: Speak you so gently? Pardon me, I pray you; I
> thought that all things had been savage here.
>
> (2.7.104–7)

The Duke's answer serves both as a repudiation of Jaques's antisocial cynicism and as a sacramental affirmation of human community:

> True is it that we have seen better days,
> And have with holy bell been knoll'd to church,
> And sat at good men's feasts, and wip'd our eyes
> Of drops that sacred pity hath engend'red;
> And therefore sit you down in gentleness,
> And take upon command what help we have
> That to your wanting may be minist'red.
>
> (2.7.120–26)

Then, immediately after Jaques's interruption, the Duke reaffirms the holy sense of mutual concern: he pointedly includes the aged Adam in the communal meal:

> Welcome. Set down your venerable burden.
> And let him feed.
>
> (2.7.167–68)

In the midst of gentleness, welcoming, help, and veneration Jaques has revealed himself as deficient in the sympathies shared by "co-mates and brothers," and is therefore finally excluded from the community achieved by comic resolution. He is not only counterbalanced, but humanized, by Touchstone; yet in a sense he is and remains more a fool than does the man in motley.

Although not so profound a creation as Lear's fool, Touchstone is clearly closely related:

> ROSALIND: Well, this is the forest of Arden.
> TOUCHSTONE: Ay, now am I in Arden; the more fool I;
>   when I was at home, I was in a better place; but travel-
>   lers must be content.
>
> (2.4.12–14)

The combination of childlike apprehension and childlike acceptance marks Lear's fool too. Moreover, in this play the fool's apprehension and acceptance upon entering the Forest of Arden are still another way of suggesting that here is a golden world manqué. Like his counterpart in *King Lear*, Touchstone speaks truer than supposedly more intelligent figures: "Thou speak'st wiser than thou art ware of," says Rosalind (2.4.53). So when he anatomizes the "seven causes" of dueling, the old Duke finds it appropriate to say, "He uses his folly like a stalking-horse, and under the presentation of that he shoots his wit" (5.4.100–101). The attack on the folly and pretense of dueling, however, is not mere random wit; dueling is a social abuse, and by making it ridicu-lous, at the end of the fifth act (compare *The Alchemist*, 4.2.67–68), Touchstone symbolically makes ridiculous all the verbal duelings and disharmonies that have occupied the inhabitants of the pastoral forest.

These duelings interweave themselves into the encounters of almost all the characters. Orlando, for instance, escapes the deadly duel with Oliver, which is made concrete by his wrestling duel with Charles, only to engage in a duel of wits with Rosalind-Ganymede, and another with Jaques. Indeed, as a recent critic has emphasized, meetings or encounters (of which such duelings are a version) substitute for conventional plot in the play's middle portion and thereby invest the action with a special lightness of tone: "such is the ease and rapidity with which pairs and groups break up, re-form, and succeed one another on the stage that there is a sense of fluid movement. All is done with the utmost lightness and gaiety, but as the lovers move through the forest, part and meet again, or mingle with the other characters in their constantly changing pairs and groups, every view of life seems, sooner or later, to find its opposite."

Such an opposition, playfully cast into dueling's artifice of thrust and riposte, is the encounter between Jaques and Orlando:

JAQUES: I thank you for your company; but, good faith, I had as lief have been myself alone.

ORLANDO: And so had I; but yet, for fashion sake, I thank you too for your society.

JAQUES: God buy you; let's meet as little as we can.

ORLANDO: I do desire we may be better strangers.

JAQUES: I pray you, mar no more trees with writing love songs in their barks.

ORLANDO: I pray you, mar no more of my verses with reading them ill-favouredly.

JAQUES: Rosalind is your love's name?

ORLANDO: Yes, just.

JAQUES: I do not like her name.

ORLANDO: There was no thought of pleasing you when she was christen'd.

JAQUES: You have a nimble wit; I think 'twas made of Atalanta's heels. Will you sit down with me? and we two will rail against our mistress the world, and all our misery.

ORLANDO: I will chide no breather in the world but myself, against whom I know most faults.

JAQUES: The worst fault you have is to be in love.

ORLANDO: 'Tis a fault I will not change for your best virtue. I am weary of you.

JAQUES: By my troth, I was seeking for a fool when I found you.

ORLANDO: He is drown'd in the brook; look but in, and you shall see him.

JAQUES: There I shall see mine own figure.

ORLANDO: Which I take to be either a fool or a cipher.

JAQUES: I'll tarry no longer with you; farewell, good Si-
    gnior Love.
ORLANDO: I am glad of your departure; adieu, good Mon-
    sieur Melancholy.

(3.2.238–77)

In such a staccato combat, the elegance of which depends on the
tension between the content of antagonism and the form of social
courtesy, both participants are rebuked for social deviance: Orlando
for his lovesickness, Jaques for his misanthropic melancholy; and each,
kept within social bounds by the form of courtesy, serves as a comic
nullifier of the other's deviance.

Neither, however, is wholly reclaimed. Jaques is never entirely
redeemed by the play's action, and Orlando is reclaimed only after
complicated and lengthy criticism by Rosalind-Ganymede. Indeed, this
comedy, even more than *Twelfth Night*, rejects romantic love as social
sickness. In the Forest of Arden romantic love replaces, and thereby
almost seems to participate in the antisocial nature of, the darker motif
of Cain against Abel that had characterized the action at court.

Orlando indicates his lovesickness by carving his emotion into the
bark of forest trees:

> O Rosalind! these trees shall be my books
> And in their barks my thoughts I'll character;
>
> . . . .
>
> Run, run, Orlando; carve on every tree
> The fair, the chaste, and unexpressive she.

(3.2.5–10)

Such a proposal echoes a motif from Virgil's pastorals:

> certum est in silvis, inter spelaea ferarum
> malle pati tenerisque meos incidere amores
> arboribus: crescent illae, crescetis, amores.

> it is certain that in the forest, among the caves of the wild
> beasts, it is better to suffer and carve my love on the young
> trees; when they grow, you will grow, my love.

The lines are from the tenth eclogue, which is where the pain of
romantic love is most specifically recognized. In *As You Like It*,
however, it is not the case that "vincit omnia Amor"; for the comic
society rebukes the pain and despair of a pastoral Gallus-like lover.

A second significance of the love-carving is that it reinforces still further the sense of Arden as something less than the pastoral ideal. Thomas Rosenmeyer, in his *The Green Cabinet: Theocritus and the European Pastoral Lyric*, points out that this "pretty vulgarism"—the "self-defeating attack upon the surface of trees"—which had its inception in Callimachus rather than in Theocritus, actually damages rather than honors the sacred environment of pure pastoral. The play makes clear, nonetheless, that the change from the motif of social sickness as brother-against-brother to the motif of social sickness as romantic love corresponds to a change from a courtly to a pastoral environment. It is, accordingly, noteworthy that Orlando's proposal to carve on the trees is directly followed by a change in the tone of Arden: it promptly becomes less an English Sherwood Forest and more a Latinate shepherd's world. As though a signal has been given, Orlando's proposal is followed by the entrance of Touchstone and of Corin, a shepherd. They duel:

> CORIN: And how like you this shepherd's life, Master
> Touchstone?
> TOUCHSTONE: Truly, shepherd, in respect of itself, it is a
> good life; but in respect that it is a shepherd's life, it
> is nought. In respect that it is solitary, I like it very well;
> but in respect that it is private, it is a very vile life.
> Now in respect it is in the fields, it pleaseth me well;
> but in respect it is not in the court, it is tedious. . . .
> Hast any philosophy in thee, shepherd?
> CORIN: No more but that I know the more one sickens the
> worse at ease he is; . . . that good pasture makes fat
> sheep; and that a great cause of the night is lack of the
> sun; . . .
> TOUCHSTONE: Such a one is a natural philosopher. Wast ever
> in court, shepherd?
> CORIN: No, truly. . . .
> TOUCHSTONE: Why, if thou never wast at court, thou never
> saw'st good manners. . . . Thou art in a parlous state,
> shepherd.
> CORIN. Not a whit, Touchstone. Those that are good man-
> ners at the court are as ridiculous in the country as
> the behaviour of the country is most mockable at court.
> (3.2.11–43)

Such extended badinage both confirms the equivocal nature of the pastoral realm in *As You Like It*, and establishes that realm as in fact pastoral. The shepherd's world is somewhat criticized as against the court; the court is somewhat criticized as against the shepherd's world.

In the shepherd's world, Orlando's love is attacked from many quarters. It is, first of all, divested of its claim to uniqueness by being ironically echoed in the pastoral lovesickness of Silvius for Phebe. It is lowered in its claim to dignity by being distortedly reflected in the bumpkin love of Touchstone for Audrey. And it is shown as a diminution, rather than a heightening, of awareness by the fact that Orlando does not know that Ganymede, to whom he laments the absence of Rosalind, is actually that Rosalind whom he so extravagantly loves. His emotion, furthermore, is made to appear moist and ludicrous by the dry criticism of Rosalind. "Then in mine own person I die," sighs Orlando. Rosalind replies:

> No, faith, die by attorney. The poor world is almost six thousand years old, and in all this time there was not any man died in his own person, videlicet, in a love-cause. Troilus had his brains dash'd out with a Grecian club; yet he did what he could to die before, and he is one of the patterns of love. Leander, he would have liv'd many a fair year, though Hero had turn'd nun, if it had not been for a hot midsummer night; for, good youth, he went but forth to wash him in the Hellespont, and, being taken with the cramp, was drown'd; and the foolish chroniclers of that age found it was—Hero of Sestos. But these are all lies: men have died from time to time, and worms have eaten them, but not for love.
>
> (4.1.82–95)

The last justly famous sentence establishes the absolute norm of comedy's rebuke to romantic love. And the invocation of Hero and Leander directs attention to Marlowe's poem. Indeed, Marlowe's antisocial life, as well as the unacceptablity of romantic love's exclusiveness, are focused by reference to Marlowe's death and by direct quotation of a line from *Hero and Leander*: "Dead shepherd, now I find thy saw of might, / 'Who ever lov'd that lov'd not at first sight?' " (3.5.80–81; *Hero and Leander*, 1.176). The question is asked, however, by the pastoral Phebe as she embarks upon a course of patent folly: blind love for Ganymede, who, in reality a woman, represents a social impossibility for the shepherdess.

Phebe's folly is underscored by her "love at first sight" infatuation; her pastoral lover, Silvius, is equally foolish, for love makes him less than a man:

> Sweet Phebe, do not scorn me; do not, Phebe.
> Say that you love me not; but say not so
> In bitterness.
>
> (3.5.1–3)

Both Phebe and Silvius are accordingly dry-beaten with Rosalind's scoff, which is the curative of such extravagant and socially unsettling emotion. To Phebe she says:

> I see no more in you than in the ordinary
> Of nature's sale-work. 'Od's my little life,
> I think she means to tangle my eyes too!
> No, faith, proud mistress, hope not after it;
> 'Tis not your inky brows, your black silk hair,
> Your bugle eyeballs, nor your cheeks of cream,
> That can entame my spirits to your worship.
>
> (3.5.42–48)

Having demolished Phebe's pretensions to uniqueness, she then turns her scorn on Silvius:

> You foolish shepherd, wherefore do you follow her,
> Like foggy south, puffing with wind and rain?
> You are a thousand times a properer man
> Than she a woman. 'Tis such fools as you
> That makes the world full of ill-favour'd children.
>
> (3.5.49–53)

Even more explicit, and much more prolonged, are the rebukes administered to Orlando. His romantic extravagance is repeatedly denigrated by being referred to in the language of sickness, and his dramatically pastoral emotion is withered by Rosalind's scorn:

> There is a man haunts the forest that abuses our young
> plants with carving "Rosalind" on their barks; hangs
> odes upon hawthorns and elegies on brambles; all, for-
> sooth, deifying the name of Rosalind. If I could meet
> that fancy-monger, I would give him some good counsel,
> for he seems to have the quotidian of love upon him.

ORLANDO: I am he that is so love-shak'd; I pray
    you tell me your remedy.
ROSALIND: There is none of my uncle's marks upon you;
    he taught me how to know a man in love; in which
    cage of rushes I am sure you are not prisoner.
ORLANDO: What were his marks?
ROSALIND: A lean cheek, which you have not; a blue eye
    and sunken, which you have not; an unquestionable
    spirit, which you have not; a beard neglected, which
    you have not. . . . Then your hose should be ungarter'd,
    your bonnet unbanded, your sleeve unbutton'd, your
    shoe untied, and every thing about you demonstrat-
    ing a careless desolation. . . .
ORLANDO: Fair youth, I would I could make thee believe I
    love. . . .
ROSALIND: But are you so much in love as your rhymes
    speak?
ORLANDO: Neither rhyme nor reason can express how
    much.
ROSALIND: Love is merely a madness. . . .
ORLANDO: I would not be cured, youth.
ROSALIND: I would cure you, if you would but call
    me Rosalind, and come every day to my cote and
    woo me.

                                       (3.2.334–92)

The artifice of Rosalind pretending to be Ganymede, and Ganymede pretending to be Rosalind again, grants the audience an insight immensely superior to that of Orlando, while equating his exaggerated love with his ignorance; and it also satisfies dramatically the idea that love is a mistaking of reality. Once love comes under the control supplied by Rosalind's criticism, however, the play begins to frolic in the dance-like patterns of *Love's Labour's Lost*. The Cain-against-Abel situation of the two dukes, like that of Orlando and Oliver, had from the first involved the play in doublings; and these, together with the doubling of Rosalind by Celia, and the Ganymede disguise by the Aliena disguise, become, as the action of the play lightens, the symmetrical doublings and repetitions of comedy's artifice. Indeed, perhaps no single place in Shakespeare's comedy achieves a more perfect coordination of symmetry, repetition, and comic inevitability than the merry-go-round of the love doctor's final social disposition of the disease of romantic love. Rosalind says to Orlando:

> Therefore, put you in your best array, bid your friends; for if you will be married tomorrow, you shall; and to Rosalind, if you will.

At this point Silvius and Phebe enter:

> PHEBE: Youth, you have done me much ungentleness.
>
> . . . .
>
> ROSALIND: I care not if I have.
>
> . . . . . .
>
> You are there follow'd by a faithful shepherd;
> Look upon him, love him; he worships you.
> PHEBE: Good shepherd, tell this youth what 'tis to love.
> SILVIUS: It is to be all made of sighs and tears;
> And so am I for Phebe.
> PHEBE: And I for Ganymede.
> ORLANDO: And I for Rosalind.
> ROSALIND: And I for no woman.
> SILVIUS: It is to be all made of faith and service;
> And so am I for Phebe.
> PHEBE: And I for Ganymede.
> ORLANDO: And I for Rosalind.
> ROSALIND: And I for no woman.
> SILVIUS: It is to be all made of fantasy.
> All made of passion, and all made of wishes;
> All adoration, duty, and observance,
> All humbleness, all patience, and impatience,
> All purity, all trial, all obedience;
> And so am I for Phebe.
> PHEBE: And so am I for Ganymede.
> ORLANDO: And so am I for Rosalind.
> ROSALIND: And so I for no woman.
> PHEBE: If this be so, why blame you me to love you?
> SILVIUS: If this be so, why blame you me to love you?
> ORLANDO: If this be so, why blame you me to love you?
>
> . . . .
>
> ROSALIND: Pray you, no more of this; 'tis like the howling
> of Irish wolves against the moon. [To Silvius] I will
> help you, if I can. [To Phebe] I would love you, if I

could.—To-morrow meet me all together. [*To Phebe*] I
will marry you if ever I marry woman, and I'll be
married to-morrow. [*To Orlando*] I will satisfy you if
ever I satisfied man, and you shall be married to-
morrow. [*To Silvius*] I will content you if what pleases
you contents you, and you shall be married to-morrow.

(5.2.66–109)

And thus the play dances to its final resolution. Hymen announces
that "Then is there mirth in heaven, / When earthly things made even
/ Atone together" (5.4.102–4), and his beautiful song pours comic
benignity lavishly over the concluding action:

> Wedding is great Juno's crown
>   O blessed bond of board and bed!
> 'Tis Hymen peoples every town;
>   High wedlock then be honoured.
> Honour, high honour, and renown,
> To Hymen, god of every town!
>
> (5.4.135–40)

The song provides one of literature's most elevated and explicit saluta-
tions to the aim and justification of comedy. Under its assurance, the
old Duke commands his society to

>   fall into our rustic revelry.
> Play, music; and you brides and bridegrooms all,
> With measure heap'd in joy, to th' measures fall.
>
> (5.4.171–73)

And yet even this comic happiness cannot totally sweeten the trace
of the bitter root in *As You Like It*. Both the usurping Duke and the
melancholy Jaques are ejected from, rather than reconciled to, the new
society. As Jaques de Boys—the new Jaques—says:

> Duke Frederick, hearing how that every day
> Men of great worth resorted to this forest,
> Address'd a mighty power; which were on foot,
> In his own conduct, purposely to take
> His brother here, and put him to the sword;
> And to the skirts of this wild wood he came,
> Where, meeting with an old religious man,
> After some question with him, was converted
> Both from his enterprise and from the world;

> His crown bequeathing to his banish'd brother,
> And all their lands restor'd to them again
> That were with him exil'd.
>
> (5.4.148–59)

And Jaques, the malcontent, is, like Molière's Alceste, equally irredeemable by the comic therapy:

> JAQUES: Sir, by your patience. If I heard you rightly,
> The Duke hath put on a religious life
> And thrown into neglect the pompous court.
> JAQUES DE BOYS: He hath.
> JAQUES: To him will I. Out of these convertites
> There is much matter to be heard and learn'd.
>
> .   .   .   .
>
> So to your pleasures;
> I am for other than for dancing measures.
>
> (5.4.174–87)

Jaques, indeed, though necessary to the process of comic catharsis in the play, has always exerted counterpressure against the pastoral ideal. When Amiens sings the lovely song that declares Arden's version of pastoral carefreeness, Jaques immediately seeks to cloud its limpidity:

> AMIENS: Under the greenwood tree
> Who loves to lie with me,
> And turn his merry note
> Unto the sweet bird's throat,
> Come hither, come hither, come hither.
> Here shall he see
> No enemy
> But winter and rough weather.
> JAQUES: More, more, I prithee more.
> AMIENS: It will make you melancholy, Monsieur Jaques.
> JAQUES: I thank it. More, I prithee, more. I can suck melancholy out of a song, as a weasel sucks eggs.
>
> (2.5.1–13)

And then Jaques produces his own song, which, in its cynicism, superimposes itself like a blotter on that of Amiens:

> If it do come to pass
> That any man turn ass,
> Leaving his wealth and ease

> A stubborn will to please,
> Ducdame, ducdame, ducdame;
> Here shall he see
> Gross fools as he,
> An if he will come to me.
>
> AMIENS: What's that "ducdame"?
> JAQUES: 'Tis a Greek invocation, to call fools into a circle.
>
> (2.5.46–56)

If the coming together of individuals into social happiness is for Jaques a calling of "fools into a circle," it is clear that his own deviation is as impervious to comic reclamation as that of the wicked younger duke.

Thus Duke Frederick and Jaques are "for other than for dancing measures," and by that fact they show that certain persisting threads of action and tone in this play are alien to the comic vision. By leaving Frederick and Jaques out of the social resolution, *As You Like It* intensifies the strain on comic limits that the villainous Don John had exerted in *Much Ado about Nothing*. That play, like this one, concludes equivocally. Benedick recites the comic benediction: "Come, come, we are friends. Let's have a dance ere we are married" (*Much Ado*, 5.4.113–14); but Don John is a loose end:

> MESSENGER: My lord, your brother John is ta'en in flight,
> And brought with armed men back to Messina.
> BENEDICK: Think not on him till to-morrow. I'll devise thee
> brave punishments for him. Strike up, pipers.
>
> (*Much Ado*, 5.4.120–24)

In *As You Like It*, Hymen's song provides a more radiant measure of comic well-being than any statements at the end of *Much Ado*, but even so the complications have moved nearer to tragedy, and Hymen cannot eradicate all the signs of strain. And after *As You Like It*, Shakespeare not only forgoes pastoral therapy for a while, but his comic vessels, leaving behind the clear waters sailed by *Twelfth Night* and *The Merry Wives of Windsor*, begin increasingly to labor in heavy seas of bitterness. The idea of the joyous society tends henceforth to be more difficult to achieve or maintain. In *The Winter's Tale*, great cracks run through the artifice of happiness, and are caulked only with difficulty. Not until *The Tempest* does Shakespeare's art, having traversed the bitter complications of the middle and late comedies, find quiet harbor in a renewed paradisal hope. There at last, in the enchanted island's golden world, the storm of cynicism and tragic disharmony, with a final rage, blows itself out.

Perspectives on Pastoral:
Romance, Comic and Tragic

Rosalie Colie

By the end of the sixteenth century, the pastoral mode embraced many particular genres, offered rich options to writers interested in literary experimentation, particularly in mixed genres, and, furthermore, had become embroiled in one of the great literary quarrels which characterized Renaissance literary theory. The pastoral permitted and encouraged opportunities for mixing in one work "imitation" with "invention," art with artifice, the artless with the artful—and generated discussions of such mixes. Eclogues were the principal pastoral form, hallowed by antiquity, but other pastoral lyrics flourished: the love-lyric, the dialogue, the song. Pastoral episodes regularly offered relief in poems largely devoted to epic gests; an English poet wrote a heroic epic in prose entitled, in spite of its relatively scant preoccupation with shepherds, *Arcadia,* and set into this prose-epic a series of pastoral poems which are themselves a self-sufficient anthology of pastoral forms and themes. Following hints from Italian eclogue-writers and fulfilling medieval Latin literary traditions, Marot and Spenser presented unabashed models of Christian pastoral, enriching the imaginative possibilities for their successors; both poets also experimented successfully with satirical poems within the pastoral mode. Indeed, one can recognize anthologies of pastoral work—Sannazaro's *Arcadia* is one example; *The Shepheardes Calender* offers a survey of pastoral themes and topics, and Sidney's shepherds in the *Arcadia* offer a magnificent epideictic display of the eclogue's range of possibilities, formal and topical.

From *Shakespeare's Living Art.* © 1974 by Princeton University Press.

From commedia dell' arte and other popular forms to the grand productions of Tasso and Guarini, drama exploited pastoral scenes, pastoral characters, and what might be called (in the Renaissance anyway) the lyric pastoral *pathétique*. The way in which the pastoral locale was taken as an official site for love-play and for love-poetry can be illustrated by a late anthology of pastoral lyrics published in 1600, *England's Helicon*; that an English Arcadian rhetoric and a mildly Arcadian logic were produced at the turn of the century shows how powerfully the literary notion of Arcadia had come to operate across the spectrum of literary possibility in England's green and pleasant land. From one end to the other of the social and literary scale, pastoral myths and patterns were available: in Whitsun pastorals, pastoral interludes, pastoral romances, in narrative books and on the stage, pastoral masques and (even more common) pastoral episodes within masques, spectators could take their pastoral experience. The ways of pastoral, then, were many and varied; the mixtures of forms, conventions, devices in pastoral allowed in very wide range of decorums.

The richness of the mixture is not really surprising: the literary critical quarrel over the pastoral as *the* mixed dramatic genre, thus as the official locus of tragicomedy, broke out over Guarini's *Il pastor fido* and culminated in the establishment of the pastoral play as the official mixture of comedy with tragedy (sometimes with satire as well), exemplified in such devices as double-plotting, mixed styles, and even interludes from the non-literary arts, such as music, dancing, and the visual arts. Wherever one looked, one could find pastoral— and once-found, twice-found, for the generous, nearly boundless forms of pastoral offered immense opportunities for craft and for imagination.

From such a background, Shakespeare's sophisticated traffic with pastoral is hardly surprising; typically, he experimented with the mode in various ways, in both early and late plays. In *As You Like It*, a play with a remarkably tight thematic construction, he worked with many pastoral themes and motifs, to say nothing of pastoral types in the dramatis personae, in what is primarily a romantic love-story derived from a prose narrative. Although "romance" and its proper subject, love, dominate this play, with the shepherding and versifying rather its decoration than its psychological locus, nonetheless the skeletal structure of this romantic comedy *is* the standard dramatic pastoral pattern—a pattern of extrusion or exile, recreative sojourn in a natural setting, with ultimate return "homeward" from the exile, a return in moral strength reinforced by the country experience of kind and kindness.

As You Like It is, for once, about sheep, but this plot-form, from academic drama to commedia dell'arte, was so thoroughly identified with the pastoral that as a formula it could imply without overtly stating a great deal of standard pastoral thematics. Sheep, for instance, were often quite absent from such plays, which sometimes lacked even the pasture environment. But the *themes* associated with pastoral (court-country, art-nature, nature-nurture) could be counted on to inform plays with this plot-pattern. A plot on this plan, thus, was a recognizable vehicle for discourse on the pastoral themes, an abstraction designed to interpret problems of nature and nurture originally associated with more overtly pastoral topics.

Though it follows the pastoral dramatic plot and has to do with sheep and shepherds, *As You Like It* is by no means "officially" pastoral. It ignores, certainly, some of the major cruces of Italian pastoral dramatic theory: it has no double-plot, for instance, in the pure sense. Though the De Boys story is separate from the ducal story, nonetheless Orlando is early displayed at court, catching the attention of Rosalind; throughout, his situation is seen as a counterpart to hers. Although the country lovers overlap with their courtly parallel figures, they are in the play rather to round out the range of pastoral alternatives than to divert into a "plot" of their own. Nor are there radical shifts of locale and of genre in *As You Like It*; the ducal and gentlemanly affairs, so to speak, are conveniently focused in one place, the forest, by means of the exile-device; though the breath of tragedy blows through the forest, the dominant tone is always, through Duke Senior's and Rosalind's efforts, kept lucidly "comic."

Duke Senior, Rosalind, Orlando: all are exiled, and in their company come the spiritual exiles who will not part from them, Celia, Touchstone, the Duke's men, Adam. In the forest these exiles, valiantly seeking some cheer, meet that symbolic, alienated, self-exiled figure, the melancholy Jaques, already located in the wood. All these victims—Jaques too—of the world find renewal in the simple culture of the Forest of Arden, and all, save Jaques and Touchstone, return triumphantly to reconstruct the social world from which they had been driven out. Against this basic construction, the play is rich in additional pastoral themes and motifs, many of them ultimately Theocritan and Vergilian, reworked throughout the Latin Middle Ages, reconceived in the Renaissance.

The play makes much of the dialogue and dialectic which so inform pastoral: the love-debates of Silvius and Corin, Silvius and

Phebe; the discussion of court and country between Corin and Touch-stone; the styles of courtship of Orlando and Rosalind; the dialogue on nature and nurture between Orlando and Oliver; and, as in Spenser's wonderful array of pastoral debates, *The Shepheardes Calender*, the themes so dialectically handled provide an enriching counterpoint to one an-other. Both the pastoral agon (Corin-Silvius) and the pastoral paragone of real sheep-herding versus literary sheep-keeping (Corin-Touchstone) are part of the play's thematic structure. Among the many things this play is, it is a comparative work about competing life-styles, among these the competition of shepherdly lives, with real shepherds who dip their sheep and lambs, whose hands smell of tar and of the oil from the sheep's wool, and others who live "poetically." We are asked to mea-sure the real and literary shepherds against each other, not once but several times. Behind the prating of the shepherd's life, important thematically as it is in the play, lies a grander anthropological concep-tion, the (pastoral) myth of the Golden World, "the antique world" in which there was perfect commerce and mutual service among men naturally well-disposed to one another, the myth, then, of the Golden Age. In antiquity, the pastoral life had been assigned to the Age of Gold, when men lived in commutual confidence and kept their flocks and herds together, their natural characters attuned to the gentle world they inhabited, their goods held comfortably and easily in common. Such a world had no need for war and was therefore an ideologically pacifist community; such discomfitures as men suffered were not caused by human agency but by natural hazards (winter and rough weather) and by creatures not yet enrolled in the peaceable kingdom (wolves and snakes, in ancient pastoral; snakes and lions in *As You Like It*; metaphorical kites and wolves and real bears in *The Winter's Tale*). Insofar as this ideal theme bears upon the dialectic of pastoral, it implies the corruption of an imperfect world of men—*urbs*, the court—against which its perfections could be fully felt.

With the development of a pastoral *pathétique* by which men identified with the gentler creatures and, in the Renaissance, allowed themselves the luxury of self-cultivation, even of emotional self-exploitation, love officially became the major pastoral occupation, taking precedence even over keeping sheep real or poetical. That is, the shepherd was naturally a poet in the pastoral genres, but before long was also a poet-lover. At first, the pastoral world was pleasant, natu-ral, easy, and so was its love—although the shepherd's complaint about his cold, coy, or faithless mistress (with a corresponding saddening of his landscape to match his emotional situation) was the celebration of another kind of love troublesome, upsetting, potentially destructive of the mutuality of pastoral society. Gradually shepherds and, later, shepherdesses began to die of love—even the pastoral landscape was not always sufficient to nourish the love-struck pastoralist through his emotional afflictions. Though the pastoral world with its celebration of timelessness and harmony would seem to have been created precisely to deny the efficacy of death, nevertheless death's shadow lay across even its green perfections to chill its warm airs.

The pastoral elegy offers a marvelous rationale for death, with its classic expression of the wonderful comforts and assuagements for personal loss; it provides the pattern for the pastoral relation of man to nature, of creation to inspiration: there, the shepherd-singer, the shepherd-maker, is gathered into the pastoral artifice of nature's eternity, these two fused into one. At one with this imaginative and nutritive nature, the dead shepherd-poet becomes a part of the inspiration he had himself once drawn from nature's store. In life poetically competitive—shepherd, goatherd, and cowherd continually sang in agon, each praising his own particular life-style, ritualized into poetic activity—and in death tradition-preserving, the pastoralist invented a world of the imagination in which, depending on his temperament, he could live as he would. He might, then, live sparingly, in simple opposition to urban luxury, confident of nature's power to provide for him; or he might live richly, feasting from nature's endless store, recreating himself and his art thereby. Whichever "nature" he chose as his setting, that entity was expected to provide sufficiently for his aesthetic and emotional needs—in other words, to nurture him.

Theocritus, with whom this all began, was less concerned with the relative values of city and country than with the positive recreations in the country: what court-country agon we find in him, we bring with us from reading subsequent pastoral writers. Vergil, however, made overt the paragone of city and country life; certainly implied in his eclogues and subsequently in the pastoral psychology is the sense of relief from the pressure of daily concerns (*negotium*) in a "liberty" and "freedom" (*otium*) consciously contrasted to the workaday round, a praise of simplicity (and, therefore, of "nature") as contrasted with the artificiality of urban life. As needs no reminder, the inventors and practitioners of literary pastoral were not professional shepherds, but highly sophisticated city-dwellers, whose country life of the imagination was quite different from that enjoyed by the inhabitants of the real

Arcadia or, after erosion, of the real Sicily. Thomas Rosenmeyer has put it well: Theocritus' Sicily is not so much a geographical place as a cartographical fiction. Even the country of Vergil's *Eclogues* is a mixed scene, by no means the recognizable North Italian locality of the *Georgics*, for instance. To call such a locale "Arcadia," Rosenmeyer tells us, is precisely to rob it of its "real" geographical implications, to insist that, as a natural spot, it is a mental artifact, a concept, an image in itself.

The encroachments of the city on the green world—of *negotium* upon *otium*—are destructive not only of a simpler form of society, but also of the psychological symbol the pastoral world is. For the literary pastoral celebrates the glorious unrealities of the imagination, its necessary furlough from its assignment of work, obligation, and duty. The iron, or at best brazen, world is man's normal portion: as Sidney put it, "poets only deliver a golden." In the literature with which we have here to deal, the literary opposition between *urbs* and *rus* shifted to become in the Renaissance a *topos* in itself, but with a particular fit to Renaissance literature and socio-economic notions—that is, it shifted its formulation from "city" to "court," and the court-country paradigm became one major focus of pastoral organization. The naturalness, freedom, delightfulness of the pastoral ethos often criticized, overtly or by implication, the self-seeking, self-aggrandizing materialistic artificiality of any court—"court" a synecdoche for any artificial, programed social organization. "Sicily" and "Arcadia" were not measured merely against (as Poggioli believed) the megalopolis, Alexandria, Rome, Paris, but against *any* strict program of social forms, formalities, polite fictions, or flatteries. At Versailles, later, queen and courtiers carried crooks and passed their time as shepherdesses and dairymaids; consciously or not, they acted out the extreme solipsism of the pastoral fiction, so delicately self-referential that only the most sophisticated can comprehend its significations. In the ambivalent symbiosis of court and country, at least in Renaissance pastoral writing, it was the courtier who came for instruction or confirmation to the shepherd, from whom the courtier, an apprentice shepherd, could learn what natural "courtesy" was.

Since the poet's world could be reshaped according to the imagination, could reject conventional decorum to set queens in the dairy, eating bread and honey, poetic imagination could work what miracles it would with its pastoral situation. If queens are dairymaids, shepherdesses can just as well be queens, or at least princesses—and so they turned out to be, over and over again, in the wish-fulfilling satisfactions of pastoral myths. The "marvelous," that subject for endless discussion among Italian critics, was commonplace in the pastoral environment, with social miracle one of pastoral's chief donations. Not least of these was the reestablishment in the pastoral environment of Golden Ageness ("poets only deliver a golden"), or (better) Golden Agelessness: in this generic country, there was no season's difference, in the forest no clock. The landscape stood, at its best, at a perpetual spring, fruiting, and harvest; at worst, the season's round was characteristically benevolent. When the landscape was not at its rich mellowness, the pastoral *pathétique* was generally to blame—the landscape had fallen off to mirror its shepherd's disappointments or depression. In this fiction, then, a poet's triumph was complete: by its means, he could create a nature whose sole poetic obligation was to identify with his emotional state. Such a nature is entirely dependent upon imaginative art, is a nature openly, proudly artificial, a nature which inverts the usual system of imitation, by which art conventionally looks to nature as its model, to offer an art form on which nature might model itself for its own improvement. The pastoral, then, offered a paradigm for the creative imagination in which the doctrine of mimesis is questioned or rejected—and so, really, is the idea of decorum. Not that the pastoral has not its own rules, conditions, and decorum—but its decorum is a conscious reversal of worldly decorus standards.

For these reasons, the art-nature question, another major critical topic of the period, was deeply tied to the pastoral mode, which became the debate's normal habitat. Poets played with the notion of pastoral nature, used as a stalking-horse against the artifices of another ethos—itself a magnificent, self-conscious artifact. From pastoral writing (often mixed with notions of education and cultivation generally classed as georgic), men took a major metaphor, that of the "improvement" of natural things, especially the improvement of breeds by crossing or grafting. "Breeding," that most natural of procedures, became an area where art counted most. The question was delightfully debated: was a man entitled to use his wit to perfect nature, or did he, by interfering in natural processes ("The Mower against Gardens"), degrade and adulterate natural patterns and products?

For agriculturalists as well as for poets speaking metaphorically, this is at once an aesthetic and a moral problem—involving, among other things, the right of the arts (all the arts, not just poetry, certainly not just pastoral poetry) to do what art does: that is, to "improve" the nature it imitates. In the simplified and rigid scheme of styles and topics inherited by Renaissance theorists ("systematized" is surely the better word), shepherds are honest people, as George Herbert put it: they speak in a simple, or low, style befitting the life they lead and the landscape in which they dwell. Should, then, kings and princesses masquerading as shepherds and shepherdesses undertake a simple style of life and of speech? What does such disguise do to a literary decorum based upon a hierarchy of values, which strict relations observed between social rank and level of style? Should those nobles who opt for the country learn, like Berowne, an uncourtly speech, doff, like Kent, the latinate orotundities of rank? Should they not, in short, suit their words to their new actions? Within the artifice of the pastoral frame, all this is made problematical, to be interestingly explored in many works. If, as countless Renaissance pastoralists demonstrate, the pastoral natural world is a complex imaginative artifice, why should not princes and princesses, with their sophisticated and finespun speech, be welcome in Arcadia, where their rhetorical finesse simply adds to the imaginative beauties in the pastoral ecology? And welcome they were—which meant that another mixture of decorums was made in this already most mixed of modes.

Such *genera mixta* bring their own contradictions. For instance, in this literary ethos so deceptively simple, the best of everything is selected: the best of genres, the best of styles, the best of solutions to human problems. No wonder then, when we seem to lose a major figure in Tasso's *Aminta* by suicide, we yet recover that figure alive by love's magic power and the accident of a convenient bush: Aminta is too valuable to be spared, and the landscape's marvels are sufficient to save even the most despairing shepherd. Art rescues men from the trials of their lives, and the pastoral makes no bones about it. No wonder, then, that as Guarini laboriously insisted against his fierce opponents and as Fletcher so gracefully observed, comedy and tragedy came so easily to dwell together in the nurturing environment of literary pastoral. Fletcher's comment on his own *Faithful Shepherdess*, written after *As You Like It* and well after the major documents of the Guarini quarrel, states the plain case for the mixture of comic and tragic modes:

> A tragie-comedie is not so called in respect of mirth and killing, but in respect it wants deaths, which is inough to make it no tragedie, yet brings some neere it, which is

inough to make it no comedie: which must be a representation of familier people with such kinde of trouble as no life
be questiond, so that a God is as lawfull in this case as in a
tragedie, and meane people as in a comedie.

Part of the reason for the tragicomic mix, then, is in the nature of the
action; another reason lies in the mixture of ranks involved in most
pastoral romances and plays, where disguise of great ones is a principal
plot-device.

With these literary or generic and social mixes, comes also moral
mixture, a mixture of ways of life set in actual or implied contradis-
tinction or even contradiction. Looking back to Theocritus, we can see
that some cultural distinction underlies the agonistic presentation of
pastoral eclogues, in the competitions between singers judged for their
skill in singing—or, to say it another way, between singers judged for
their success in defending their particular variant upon the pastoral life.
Neatherd, goatherd, shepherd challenged one another, to be challenged
in turn by fishermen and mowers, sometimes even by huntsmen—and,
given such a thoroughly country mixture, why not by a courtier as
well, especially a courtier disguised as a countryman? Of course, by
the time we arrive at this particular elaboration of pastoral agon, a
radical discharge of original pastoral democracy has been effected:
when court invades country, rank, however understressed, intrudes
upon such egalitarian commutuality as countrymen enjoy, alters the
condition in which, as the Golden Age myth had it, social class was
irrelevant. Once the mixture of class is accepted in the pastoral system,
then alienation may become a conscious topic, too: perhaps this is
Vergil's point in the First Eclogue. So the melancholy Jaques may not
be all that out of place in the Forest of Arden, even though he is
"Monsieur Traveler" and, it would seem, at the very least a university
wit. He has, presumably, become disgusted and worn out by the
conflicting sophistications he has seen and is, at least, true to the Arden
he criticizes, when alone of the cast he declines to return to court.
Celia's choice of pseudonym, Aliena, honors the reason for her voluntary exile and is one token of her courtier-status within the forest. The
pastoral world is not for the disappointed and victimized alone, to
relearn their integrity; it exists also for those more seriously estranged
from society, as the early reference in *As You Like It* to Robin Hood
suggests.

II

As You Like It miraculously collects the major themes of the pastoral, manipulating and juxtaposing them so as to bring that rich mix under critical scrutiny. Not only is the classic pastoral dramatic pattern its basic fiction—exile from court; country restoration; triumphant return to court—but so also are the themes of nature and nurture, of art and nature, of art and artifice, of court and country debated in eclogue-like exchanges uttered by representatives of pastoral and non-pastoral (sometimes even anti-pastoral) positions. The "parallel and parody" of the play, so well analyzed by Jay Halio and others, works beautifully to undermine doctrinaire attitudes, social, moral, or literary. The play's perspectivism is sufficient exposure of the implications of the *vie sentimentale* for which pastoral had come so masterfully to stand.

Even satire and folly, embodied in Jaques and Touchstone, in turn set into agon, come to challenge and to reinforce the values of this pastoral. The love at the center of the play is not a particularly pastoral love, save in that the playwright works toward eliminating the artificial and nonnatural aspects and elements of love; but the pastoral tradition, with its exquisite concentrations upon the emotional nuances and values of love, offered a superb literary opportunity for examining the love-subject.

Nor is love the only topic so scrutinized: Corin speaks of his content in the life he leads, in open contrast to Touchstone's obvious dependency upon his ladies, yet we know from his own mouth that Corin is shepherd to another man and not, in Fletcher's sense, one of the true literary shepherds who are "owners of flockes and not hyerlings." Corin qualifies his own position: so does Touchstone who, praising the court above the shepherd's life, by his witty chop-logic lays open the shabbiness of the court's customs. Shepherd and jester are brothers, after all, under the skin: Touchstone, remembering Jane Smile, recalls that early love in the generic language of the peasant Corin. The "country copulatives" comment on each other, and on the courtiers: Orlando, courtly mock-shepherd genuinely disinherited, dotes on Rosalind; Silvius, a real shepherd who has learned his love-role as thoroughly as Orlando has his, dotes upon Phebe; Phebe, a real shepherdess struck by the *coup de foudre* prescribed by Marlowe (to whom they refer as "the dead shepherd," in pure literary idiom), dotes upon Ganymede; and Ganymede dotes, as he insists, upon no woman.

All of them, even the trim Ganymede, smugly apart from their encirclement, show some aspects of pastoral loving; all of them, in turn, have been called (like all fools) into a circle. Ganymede assumes with his disguise (Shakespeare's one-upmanship is manifest in this boy-actor-disguised-as-a-girl-disguised-as-a-boy-acting-the-part-of-a-girl) one proper pastoral love-attitude, that conventionally assigned the shepherdess, of coolness to the lover. Orlando may not have been given a gentleman's education by his hard-hearted brother, but he knows all the same that proper pastoral lovers hang poems on trees. Silvius loves his lady totally, as if she were perfectly beautiful, in spite of Rosalind's rebuke to Phebe; and Phebe illustrates, before our very eyes how totally love can wipe out all other considerations, particularly those of common sense.

Yet all shall be changed: though in the beginning each loves the wrong person, we see Phebe settle for Silvius; we see Touchstone, clad in his courtly aura as well as in motley, win the goatgirl Audrey from the well-to-do rural William—win her, then, by his courtly "rank." We see Aliena paired with the repentant Oliver, both of them struck as finally as Phebe by Marlovian love at first sight. And we see, by a magic attributable to her forest-character, Ganymede-Rosalind claim her lover Orlando. Only Silvius and Phebe, of the whole crowd, are what they seem and no more: the others, one way or another, have been disguised from others and from themselves. And all of them, save Silvius and Phebe, must cope with the undisguising: Audrey must be either taken to the court by her fool or brutally abandoned: Aliena-become-Celia at once threatens her lover's recent vow of shepherdhood, that sign of his reconciliation with kind nature; Orlando must learn what his beloved is to inherit.

Desengaño does not rob the pastoral of its sweetness in As You Like It. These considerations do not intrude upon the play itself, in which, however much pastoral love is mocked, its sweet fidelities are rewarded, too. By making fun of Orlando's language, Rosalind jokes him into ever-increasing avowals of his love for her. She may seem to mock all lovers, but at the news of Orlando's hurt by the lion faints like a green girl. Touchstone does not want to be in Arden and contrasts Corin's life unfavorably with what he had known at the court, but he makes the best of his forest opportunities, and his logic actually recoils on him, to endorse the simplicities Corin embodies. The melancholy-satiric Jaques comes to scoff at pastoral sentimentalism, but he is scoffed at in his turn—and for pastoral sentimentalism at that. The data of various literary modes are mocked and yet, through all the mockery, reaffirmed: questioned, teased, tested, found wanting—and found valuable in spite of manifest weaknesses.

In this way, perspectivism is built into the play; it is the play's method, but it relies on traditional implications within the mode, by developing an inherent dialectical tendency in pastoral eclogues to an astonishing degree. Many contests question the traditions which ultimately they endorse: the lovers' fourfold catch suggests the merry-go-round illusion of the experience of loving; Corin and Silvius speak not just about love, but about the kinds of love appropriate to the different ages of man, and Jaques deals with love as developmental folly in his far more total indictment of man's ages and the illusions of each age. Touchstone and Corin debate the life of court and country to demonstrate the limitations of both. Jaques marches through the play, in his melancholy isolation a challenge to everyone's social assumptions and conclusions: like Philisides, Sidney's name for his symbolic self in the *Arcadia*, Jaques has retired to the forest in disappointment with the world's offerings. Though established in Arden, Jaques is characterized as a traveler, a continentalized Englishman who (as the character-books assure us) can never find aught at home good again. He is also—a bit unexpectedly—the superpastoralist of the play, speaking out for the pathetic identification of creatural suffering with human unhappiness. He it is who criticizes the Robin Hood band of gentlemen around Duke Senior for their unbrotherly attacks upon the deer-commonwealth, whose "fat burghers" are slaughtered for men's whims and pleasure; but all this while he is also unpastorally melancholy, unpastorally antisocial. As we look at him more narrowly, of course, we see the social role his melancholy fulfills, and how consistently Jaques acts the part of the Duke's men expect of him. It is he who recognizes a freedom even greater than that of the forest in his cry, "Motley's the only wear!" He knows how to call all fools into a circle; he, in short, reminds us by most unpastoral means that Arden is a pleasaunce, that for all its rough weather, the forest is also Cockayne, where all is upside down to be set aright. He knows what his fellow-fool recognizes at sight: "Ay, now I am in Arden; the more fool I; when I was at home I was in a better place; but travellers must be content." And yet Arden is his home, as he chooses to remain in the forest now solitary enough for his nature.

What the forest is, is never made entirely clear, although it *is* obvious that, even with the season's difference, the forest is a better place than the usurper's court. In the forest there is no need for "new

news o' the new court"; fashionable gossip is irrelevant to the fundamental constants of courtesy, civility, and humanity. And yet, for all
the talk of the golden world, Arden is never "really" that—Corin's
master was of churlish disposition and inhospitable, ready to sell his
sheepfarm for gold. Unprofessional cleric that he is, Sir Oliver Martext
is nonetheless at home in Arden; Duke Senior's fellow exiles do not
hesitate to comment on the bitter wind, painful to them if less "un-
kind" than man's ingratitude. The moral arrangements of the golden
world are, come wind come weather, scrupulously observed, together
with the pastoral delusions. The melancholy Jaques is courteously
received, his idiosyncrasies are respected, enjoyed, and even admired;
when Orlando, assuming the role of salvage man, bursts in upon the
fête champêtre, he is welcomed, not repulsed, in spite of his words and
his sword; the country lovers ultimately accept each other with grace.
The Duke lives, "the Robin Hood of England" to whom young
gentlemen flock "every day, and fleet the time carelessly," so that such
rank as he has is, like Robin Hood's, only first among equals. To the
forest come Rosalind and Celia, Touchstone faithfully in attendance; to
the forest comes Jaques; to the forest comes the outlawed Orlando,
with old Adam on his back. In the forest Oliver de Boys and Duke
Frederick make their moral recoveries and find their various rewards.
In the forest, the fairy-tale world rules: a serpent and a lion, hitherto
inconceivable, threaten the only newcomer distinguished for his savagery: in token of his recognition of the beast within, Oliver had
become a hairy man. In Arden, an untaught innocent younger-brother-
hero can save that newcomer from these creatures by the "kindness"
of his "nature," which marks him as trueborn in spite of his deprivation of nurture. In the forest, whatever nature's natural drawbacks,
nature makes written calendars irrelevant: there are no clocks in the
forest, and there is time enough for everyone's inner and social needs:
the forest, as C. L. Barber reassuringly claims, induces and confirms
holiday humor.

Time does not pass, theoretically at least, in the golden world—but
this rule does not hold for our play, where we are endlessly made
aware, both in earnest and in jest, of the passage of time: in the
confrontation of generations (Silvius and Corin, dukes and daughters,
Sir Rowland's sons and his aged servant Adam); Orlando comes late to
his appointments with Ganymede, who rates him for that—because
she is a younger girl in love, as she tells us in her psychological
typology of time, time trots hard with her. A living emblem of the last

age of man, the nearly dying Adam is brought in to emphasize Jaques's classic oration. In other words, this forest is at once ideal and real; the inhabitants of Arden insist that their life is unvaried, as in the Golden Age; but the play works in the rhythms of experience's human actuality. On one side, Arden *is* holiday, and thus timeless; it offers a chance for recovery and redemption, a parodic, exalted imitation of the real world, now corrected and purged. In Arden, fools are visibly in circles, men feast graciously on venison and wine—but time passes as they do so, as we are continually reminded, and men ripen and rot in spite of the lack of clocks.

What the forest offers is its liberties: love finds what it seeks; Jaques is allowed to criticize as he likes; Touchstone may mock, Corin may be threatened with impoverishment. But nothing untoward happens; the forest offers restitution to the dispossessed as well as the far more important imaginative freedom in which the natural spirits of men and women may expand. Duke Senior, Rosalind, and Orlando know that this forest is their goal; there they find a world where even real brothers can be brothers. For with the psychological flowering favored in Arden, we are reminded that all life is not so free: Cain and Abel patterns recur in the play, in each generation. Even in *that* pattern, indeed, one can find a pastoral analogue: the pastoral Abel is the contemplative man, Cain the cultivator, the active man, the man of violence prepared to defend the value of his way of life and its produce. In his underpopulated world, Cain felt he had to savage his brother, as Duke Frederick and Oliver seek to savage their brothers. When these romance-brothers enter the forest, however, reformation strikes at once; the virtuous maintain and corroborate their gentility and their gentleness, and the evil recover or discover the gentleness in themselves they had denied. Orlando's lapse into savagery, so clearly motivated by his concern for old Adam, is immediately reversed by the gentleness with which his threat of violence is received. As is usual in these discussions of pastoral nature, we find throughout the play the terms which form its structure: nature, natural, kind, kindness, civil, civility, gentle, and gentleness. For nature is kind, and kindness: a recognition of one's kind, a response designed to protect and to strengthen whatever is mutually human.

Against this background, Orlando's complaint against his unnatural nurture makes fell sense. His brother owed him, as kin, to raise him as the gentleman he is, but chose instead to rob him of his rights and to cast him, if he could, as a type of Prodigal Son. Finally, Oliver even tried to kill the boy, in an unmotivated gesture of the supreme unkindness. Oliver is presented, as Iago was to be, as simply evil—"simply" evil. The question of nature and nurture running through so much of the play is nowhere debated outright, but from the start the debaters are given real parts in the play. In contrast to his brother, Orlando is, as his behavior consistently confirms, preternaturally "gentle," even though he is also preternaturally strong. Actually, as he and we come to recognize, he has no need of that mysterious education he laments, and grows into a symbolic portion far grander than his inheritance would have been. Orlando assumes responsibility for Adam, grown old in his father's service, to the extent that he violates his own nature by attempting to steal for his sake. He cannot pass by on the other side and let the lion attack his sleeping brother, for all that his brother has done against him. His natural qualities caused him to fall in love with Rosalind, and her to fall in love with him. He speaks of his own gentility ("Yet am I inland bred") and recognizes the same "inland" quality in Ganymede's speech, anomalously cultured for the child of the forest he claims to be. Folk hero that he is, Orlando, the youngest of three sons, is eminently suited to take his place at the head of his family and to marry the Duke's daughter at the end of the play, to return with daughter and Duke to the court, confident of exhibiting the courtliness he has always naturally displayed.

The debate between nature and nurture overlaps the problem of nature and art: nurture is education, altering, improving, grafting, conventionally taken as "good." In Orlando's case, it turns out that the art of which he laments the lack is in fact superfluous. He is what he is "by nature"—and when he assumes various stylized, courtly poses, such as in his role of pastoral lover, Rosalind makes fun of his efforts. As often happens in Shakespeare's versions of pastoral, the nature-nurture debate is skewed and ultimately denied, as received dialectical opposites are shown to be fused in the person (Orlando, Perdita, Arviragus, Guiderius) whose gentle birth marches with his courteous nature. Nurture is not necessary for such as these: all the education in the world had failed to improve Oliver, until he experienced his brother's miraculous assertion of kindness. In Jaques, we see that education has even weakened his feelings for his kind. Rosalind is not the nutbrown boy she pretends she is; her cultivated ancestry of magicians is a fiction to account for the cultivation of her nature and her breeding. In her case, indeed, the disguise which makes it possible for her to take her place in Arden is a fiction in itself. Though she is spokeswoman for what is natural, real, and psychologically sincere, and persuades Orlando to natural and unstylized love, she is of course always neither simple nor boy.

The forest, then, shelters a countersociety, idyllic and playful, offering a model of possibility to the real world, a countersociety made up on the one hand by the fictions of a literary convention and on the other by the types of that convention, determined to express the goodness of their natures. The pastoral second chance offered by the Forest of Arden is not just a second chance for the people in the play; it is equally a second chance for the larger society of which the *dramatis personae* are representatives. As the procession troops courtward, men with antlers on their heads, girls dressed as country brother and sister, nutbrown from sun or dye, dukes and reconciled brothers, we believe in the escapade and in their unlikely return, believe in their capacity to maintain reform, because of the upright good sense they have demonstrated or learned in the forest, because of their natural courtesy, kindness, and radiant moral strength. But we believe in them also because the pastoral refuge has acknowledged the flawed realities of the working day world; the holiday has recognized real experience. Touchstone is not the only character on whom the truth of experience can be proved: all of them try, assay, essay the pastoral myth, each from his own perspective, and all of them find at its heart the recreative values of nature, kind, and kindness promised by the tradition. The play's perspectivism insists also upon the convergence of all views at its central and controlling point, the symbolic, simple truth of this most artificial of literary constructs.

Existence in Arden

Ruth Nevo

The two great comedies composed during the last years of the sixteenth century share many features which place them in something of a
class apart. One of these is the confident, even demonstrative noncha-
lance with which they relate to the Terentian tradition. It is as if
Shakespeare reaches his majority in them, knows it, and would have us
know it. It is almost as if we hear him indulging in a sly joke about the
whole paternalistic New Comedy model when he has Rosalind, at
some undramatized point, meet her father in the forest, where, as she
later reports to Celia, she had much question with him: "He ask'd me
of what parentage I was. I told him of as good as he, so he laugh'd and
let me go. But what talk we of fathers, when there is such a man as
Orlando?" (3.4.36–39). With no parental obstacles, no separating mis-
prisions or vows or oaths, with no reason (as has often been pointed
out) for Rosalind's continuing disguise once she is safe in the forest and
the writer of the execrable verses identified, *As You Like It* is the only
comedy in which the two chief protagonists fall in love not as victims
of blind Cupid, or of plots of one kind and another, or against their
own conscious will, but freely, open-eyed, reciprocally and as if in
godsent fulfilment of their own deepest desires.

Their meeting is finely, appropriately rendered. Orlando is hesi-
tant, disconcerted, incredulous, speechless; Rosalind responds with the
immediate joyful, irrepressible spontaneity of her confession to Celia.
Some of *her* speechlessness, she says, is "for my child's father" (1.3.2).

From *Comic Transformations in Shakespeare*. © 1980 by Ruth Nevo. Methuen, 1980.

But this is a comic ending (or very near ending), rather than a comic beginning; and indeed the whole carriage of the play seems almost to set the comedy sequence on its head. The grave potential dangers are concentrated at the start, the tangle of mistaken identities occurs as late as the end of act 3.

"What," indeed, asks Barber, "is the comedy in *As You Like It* about? What does Shakespeare ridicule? At times one gets the impression that it doesn't matter very much what the characters make fun of so long as they make fun." Sandwiched between *Much Ado* and *Twelfth Night*, Harold Jenkins notes:

> *As You Like It* is conspicuously lacking in comedy's more robust and boisterous elements—the pomps of Dogberry and the romps of Sir Toby . . . [and] it has nothing which answers to those bits of crucial trickery . . . which link events together by the logical intricacies of cause and effect. *As You Like It* takes Shakespearean comedy in one direction nearly as far as it could go before returning (in *Twelfth Night*) to a more orthodox scheme.

The point is very well taken. The play exhibits not only a different direction but a markedly looser and more casual handling of the "orthodox scheme," which I take to mean the Terentian formula; and it is this which makes inspired improvisation, the capacity to seize and make the most of one's opportunities, a key factor in the comic remedy itself. That which is therapeutic to the human condition is elicited here too by considerable anxiety and error, is winnowed clear of delusion and snatched by a hair's breadth from disaster. But what is prominently displayed, extruded, so to speak, as surface structure in *As You Like It* is the wisdom / folly dialectic of comedy itself, as antinomies are first exacerbated and then transcended. And what it embodies in its trickster heroine is comic pleasure itself, in practice and in action: a liberating playful fantasy, an expansive reconciliation of opposites of all kinds, enlivening and enchanting, to be enjoyed and rejoiced in; a heaven-sent euphoria. It is a play so self-assured as not to care whether we notice or not that it is talking about its own mode of being. It is a meta-comedy, in which the underlying principles of Shakespearean practice are drawn out for all to see and turned into the comic material itself.

The play polarizes harm and remedy in its initial catalogue of imperfections and deficiencies—the most dire we have yet encountered—

and in the flight of its refugees. A youngest son seeks his proper place
in the world. His elder brother keeps him rustically at home, like a
peasant, breeds his horses better—they are not only fed but taught—
allows him nothing but mere growth and, in short "mines his gentility
with his education." For this servitude becomes unendurable. Orlando
knows no wise remedy, and there begins his sadness. Elsewhere in the
kingdom a duke is displaced by his younger brother and flees into
exile, leaving his daughter mourning his absence. A thug is hired to
dispatch the rebellious younger brother under cover of a court wrestling match, and when the plan miscarries, the young man and his
faithful retainer are unceremoniously turned out to make their way in
the world as best they can. The usurping duke, unable to bear the
accusing presence of his elder brother's daughter banishes her the court
on pain of death. "Thou art a fool," he says to his daughter, her
friend, who entreats him to let her stay:

> She is too subtile for thee, and her smoothness,
> Her very silence, and her patience
> Speak to the people, and they pity her.
> Thou art a fool; she robs thee of thy name,
> And thou wilt show more bright and seem more virtuous
> When she is gone.
>
> (1.3.77–82)

His counterpart, Oliver, has a similar message concerning folly to
deliver to his younger brother: "What will you do, you fool," he says,
in effect, "when you have the meagre pittance your father left you?
Beg when that is spent?"

This is the cold world of Edmund and Goneril in which there is
no place for goodness and virtue, no room for undissimulated feeling;
the tainted, radically corrupt world of court or city, of lust for gain
and place, of craft and deceit. From wicked brother and wicked uncle
there is no recourse for the oppressed but to take flight, which they do
gladly. They go "To liberty, and not to banishment." (1.2.138), to
"some settled low content" (2.3.68) as they say in their worldly folly,
and arrive by a providential coincidence in the same wood, with
nothing but their natural loyalty and generosity, their foolish good
nature, and love, contracted at the wrestling match. Back home,
cunning and treachery—called worldly wisdom—grow ever more manifest under the impetus of their own accumulation. This is rendered
with a splendid acid brevity in act 3, scene 1, when Oliver declares his

kinship to Duke Frederick in the matter of affection for his wayward brother Orlando:

> OLIVER: O that your Highness knew my heart in this! I
>   never lov'd my brother in my life.
> DUKE FREDERICK: More villain thou. Well, push him out of
>   doors,
>   And let my officers of such a nature
>   Make an extent upon his house and lands.
>
> (3.1.13–17)

The exposition of *As You Like It* presents a whole society in need of cure, not a temporary emergency, or lunacy, to be providentially set right.

Since this is the case, however, a good deal of manoeuvring is required to keep the play within the orbit of comedy. The source story in Lodge is far fiercer—there are several deaths; but even Shakespeare's toning down of the violence, and a reduction of the casualties to Charles's broken ribs is not sufficient to make the initiating circumstances mere harmless aberrations, or, at worst, aberrations which only an accumulation of mishaps and ill fortune will render disastrous. To transform the Lodge story into comedy, therefore, necessitated a shift of gear, and the production of what one might call a second order set of follies from the realm not of the reprehensible but of the ridiculous; a modulation from vice to error, and potentially liberating error at that. It is the flight into the forest during the long second act which effects this transformation.

The flight into the forest draws upon the tradition of that other time and other place of the nostalgic imagination—the *locus amoenus* where the return to nature from corrupt civilization allows the truth, simplicity and humility of innocence to replace the treachery, craft and arrogance of worldly sophistication. But the audience, following the courtiers in their flight from usurpation, cruelty, artifice and deceit discover in the forest the usurpation of Corin, the boorish rusticity of Audrey and William and the factitious elegancies of imitation courtly love masking sexual tyranny in the shepherd lovers; while, before the story is over, the forest's lionesses and snakes will have revealed in it possibilities no less inhospitable, not to say predatory, than those of the vicious court.

What we perceive is a plethora of disjunctive contraries. The whole of act 2 bandies views of the good life about between defendants of court and country respectively, in a battery of claims and counter-claims which turns each into its opposite, revealing the absurdity of polarized and partial solutions. Shakespeare erects a burlesque dialectic during which, at every point, assumptions are refuted by realities and opinions fooled by facts.

Amiens sings to whoever

doth ambition shun,
And loves to live i' the' sun,
(2.5.38–39)

promising him no enemy but winter and rough weather. The disenchanted Jaques, whom there is no pleasing, caps Amiens's with another stanza (or stanzo–Jaques cares not for their names since they owe him nothing) pointing out that anyone who leaves his hearth and ease is an ass, and will find nothing but fools as gross as he in the greenwood. And Amiens's second song is less buoyant about winter and rough weather, not to mention friendship and loving, than the first.

Orlando, who has no illusions about "the uncouth forest" swears to succour the fainting Adam: if there be anything living in the desert, he says, "I will either be food for it, or bring it for food to thee." It is as succinct a summary of nature red in tooth and claw as may be found, but oddly enough Orlando, who complained of the poverty of Nature, denied the benefits of Nurture, steeling himself for savagery, finds civility in the forest. "Your gentleness shall force. / More than your force moves us to gentleness," says the Duke, his rhetorical chiasmus figuring the contraries. More precisely: figuring the contraries resolved in a way that is characteristic, as we shall see, of the Duke.

According to the melancholy Jaques that "poor dappled fool" the deer, who has his "round haunches gored" in his own native "city" is a standing reproach to all seekers of the good life in the forest. But Jaques's bleak account of human ageing in the seven ages speech (2.7.139ff.) is immediately refuted by Orlando's tender care for an old and venerable faithful servant. Jaques's various orations "most invectively" pillory not only country, city and court, but "this our life" in its entirety (2.1.58). But Jaques's view that evil is universal and good an illusion is countered from yet another perspective by Touchstone's: that folly is universal and wisdom an illusion.

These two represent the play's opposing poles, but in asymmetrical opposition. They are a teasingly complex instance of Shakespeare's fools, referred to [previously]. The meeting between them is reported exultantly be Jaques in act 2, scene 7, with much rejoicing, on the part of that arrogant nihilist, in the capacity for metaphysics of a mere fool. But the audience is quietly invited to perceive that there is an extraordinary similarity between Touchstone's oracular ripening and rotting and Jaques's own disenchanted rhetoric, and we are invited to wonder whether it is not after all the ironical fool who is mocking, by parody, the philosophical pretensions of the sentimental cynic. The scene plays handy dandy (like Lear) with the question most germane to comedy (as Lear's to tragedy): which is the Eiron, which the Alazon? Which is the mocker and which the mocked? Who is fooling and who is fooled?

What after all does Touchstone *not* mock? He dismantles, systematically and with detached amusement, the entire structure of syllogistic reasoning with which his betters occupy their minds:

> Truly shepherd, in respect of itself, it is a good life; but in respect that it is a shepherd's life, it is naught. In respect that it is solitary, I like it very well; but in respect that it is private, it is a very vild life. Now in respect it is in the fields, it pleaseth me well; but in respect it is not in the court, it is tedious. As it is a spare life (look you) it fits my humor well; but as there is no more plenty in it, it goes much against my stomach. Hast any philosophy in thee, shepherd?
>
> (3.2.13–22)

A premise, to Touchstone is nothing but its own potential contrary, as he delights to demonstrate with his mock or anti-logic of all's one:

> That is another simple sin in you, to bring the ewes and the rams together, and to offer to get your living by the copulation of cattle; to be bawd to a bell-wether, and to betray a she-lamb of a twelve-month to a crooked-pated old cuckoldly ram, out of all reasonable match.
>
> (3.2.78–83)

Nevertheless, Touchstone is a fool. Audrey is there to remind us of that. And so what we come to see is that both monistic or polarized solutions—that evil is universal and good an illusion, and that folly is universal and wisdom an illusion are being mocked.

However, the play makes it clear which it prefers, which it includes, finally. It finds a place—a key place, as we shall see—for the mother wit which Touchstone demonstratively parades, and parodies. It is Jaques, totally lacking in good humour, who is sent packing. First by the Duke, in terms which are significant, in view of comedy's concern with remedies for human ills. The Duke checks Jaques's enthusiasm about cleansing with satire the foul body of the infected world with the command, Physician, heal thyself:

> Most mischievous foul sin, in chiding sin:
> For thou thyself hast been a libertine,
> As sensual as the brutish sting itself;
> And all th' embossed sores, and headed evils,
> That thou with license of free foot hast caught,
> Would'st thou disgorge into the general world.
>
> (2.7.64–69)

And then by the lovers. "I thank you for your company, but, good faith, I had as lief have been myself alone" is Jaques's opening ploy when he meets Orlando. He doesn't, it transpires, approve of Orlando's verse, of his love's name, of his "pretty answers" (probably "conn'd out of rings"), of his "nimble wit" at which he learnedly sneers, of his being fool enough to be in love at all. What he would like to do, he says, is to sit down and "rail against our mistress the world, and all our misery." At the end of this dispiriting conversation Orlando sends him to seek the fool he was looking for in the brook (3.2.253–93 passim). And Rosalind, similarly tried by Jaques's disquisition on his own unique and inimitable brand of melancholy, would "rather have a fool to make [her] merry than experience to make [her] sad—and travel for it too!" (4.1.28).

If (much virtue in "if")—if we must choose between disjunctions, too cool a head is evidently preferable to too cold a heart. But must we choose? Certainly act 2 (in particular) with its reiterated pastoral polemic, its multitude of syntactic, imagistic, situational figurations of either / or places us constantly in attitudes of indecision, or of quasi-dilemma. Nothing is happening, of course, so that these are not the impossible choices of tragic action; they are merely virtual. These constantly collapsing or exploding solutions of the greenwood constitute the comic disposition which the process of the play heightens and mocks. The characters all have answers to the question of the good life, but their answers keep being refuted; keep being invaded by aspects of reality they have not taken into account. Yet they continue tirelessly searching. Moreover, the comedy of this second act is an almost Chekovian dialogue of the deaf. Everybody is talking philosophically about life. Ah Life. But it is only themselves they really hear. The Duke, who needs grist for his mill, loves, he tells us, to cope Jaques in his sullen fits, for "then he's full of matter." But Jaques, who has no patience with another's problems, has been trying all day to avoid him: "He is too disputable for my company," says he, with sardonic derision. "I think of as many matters as he, but I give heaven thanks, and make no boast of them" (2.5.35–37).

If then disjunctive logic is the comic disposition in Arden (reflecting the disjunction of good and evil in the play's outer frame), any remedy will have to mediate or bridge the fissuring of human experience which is thus symbolized. It is the good Duke (meta-*senex* for a meta-comedy?) who points the way to such a resolution.

The Duke's stoicism is more than a brave show. His speech (2.1.1–17) on the sweet uses of adversity and the preferability of biting winter winds to man's ingratitude and the ingratiation of court sycophancy is a profoundly dialectical *concordia discors*, transcending, with its paradoxes, diametrical contraries. He is, it is to be noted, as aware as Jaques of the universality of evil. It is he who first notices the anomaly of the deer hunt, though it is Jaques who rubs it in. He does not say that Arden is a rose garden. He only says that he recognizes the penalty of Adam. Duke Senior does not deny the icy fangs of the winter wind, the ugly venom of the toad. On the contrary, he welcomes them because they "feelingly persuade him what he is." The contraries: painted pomp and icy fangs; chiding and flattery; feeling and persuasion (intuition and reason, we would say); books and brooks; sermons and stones, are all resolved in his remedial vision of the good life to be found in the hard discipline of nature, not in her soft bosom; in the riches of deprivation, not in the poverty of prodigality. "Happy is your Grace," says Amiens, "That can translate the stubbornness of fortune / "Into so quiet and so sweet a style" (2.1.18–20).

This Duke is indeed wise enough to be Rosalind's father but his wisdom of retreat, his embracing of penury, does not nurture a comic economy which requires bonus and liberating excess. He is the ideologue of resolutions, not their protagonist. Nor is the virtue that he makes of dispossession entirely victorious. They are doing their best, these exiles, to keep their spirits up, and there are moments of greenwood merriment, to be sure, but it doesn't take much to set off in them a yearning for better days. When the young man rushes on with his drawn sword shouting for food, and meets the Duke's courteous welcome, he also poignantly reminds him of the privations of a purely private virtue:

> what e'er you are
> That in this desert inaccessible,
> Under the shade of melancholy boughs,
> Lose and neglect the creeping hours of time;
> If ever you have look'd on better days,
> If ever been where bells have knoll'd to church,
> If ever sate at any good man's feast,
> If ever from your eyelids wip'd a tear,
> And know what 'tis to pity, and be pitied,
> (2.7.109–17)

The Duke echoes his sentiments with enthusiasm, and invites him to a meal served with as ducal a propriety as circumstances permit. The Duke can do much, but *As You Like It* requires, for its proper centre, his daughter. Which brings us to the lovers.

While the veteran refugees are thinking of many matters, these newcomers are thinking of one alone. Orlando, so far from finding settled low content in the forest, finds a compulsion to dream of fair women and to publish his poetasting upon every tree; and Rosalind, who had seized the opportunity, while she was about it, to satisfy a girl's tomboy fantasies:

> Were it not better,
> Because that I am more than common tall,
> That I did suit me all points like a man?
> A gallant curtle-axe upon my thigh,
> A boar-spear in my hand, and—in my heart
> Lie there what hidden woman's fear there will—
> We'll have a swashing and a martial outside,
> As many other mannish cowards have
> That do outface it with their semblances.
> (1.3.114–22)

now finds an echo to her own thoughts in the lovelorn Silvius. "Alas, poor shepherd searching of [thy wound], / I have by hard adventure found my own" is her sympathetic response to Silvius's plaint (2.4.44–45ff.). The meeting precipitates the process of self-discovery which the comic device in act 2, the disguise whereby Rosalind both reveals and conceals her true identity, will infinitely advance.

"Arcadia," says Peter Marinelli [in *Pastoral*] (and the perceptive remark applies as well to Arden), "is a middle country of the imagination . . . a place of Becoming rather than Being, where an individual's potencies for the arts of life and love and poetry are explored and tested." Shakespeare's Arcadia offers a further turn: his comic heroine's own potencies for the arts of life and love and poetry are explored and tested by a variety of contingencies even while she is testing and exploring these same potencies in others.

Her initial absence of mind at the first encounter with Silvius is amusingly rendered by her failure to take in Touchstone's derisive parody of fancy shepherds:

> I remember when I was in love, I broke my sword upon a stone, and bid him take that for coming a-night to Jane Smile; and I remember the kissing of her batler and the cow's dugs that her pretty chopp'd hands had milk'd; and I remember the wooing of a peascod instead of her, from whom I took two cods, and giving her them again, said with weeping tears, 'Wear these for my sake'.
>
> (2.4.46–54)

All she hears, and that inattentively, is his epigrammatic ending: "as all is mortal in nature, so is all nature in love mortal in folly." Upon which she sagely replies, "Thou speak'st wiser than thou art ware of," and misses again entirely the fool's iron snub. "Nay, I shall ne'er be ware of mine own wit till I break my shins against it" (2.4.58–59).

But this is the last time Rosalind is inattentive or absentminded. Indeed it is her presence of mind which dominates and characterizes the middle acts.

From the moment when she finds herself trapped in her page role and exclaims in comic consternation, "Alas the day, what shall I do with my doublet and hose?" to the moment of her unmasking, Ganymede releases in Rosalind her best powers of improvisation, intuition, and witty intelligence. Her quick wit transforms her page disguise into the play's grand comic device, and turns comic predicament to triumphant account. When she says to Celia: "Good my complexion, doest thou think, though I am caparison'd like a man, I have a doublet and hose in my disposition? One inch of delay more is a South-sea of discovery." (3.2.194–97), her gift for comic hyperbole as well as her ironic self-awareness are delightfully in evidence. But the master invention of the play lies in "the inch of delay more" which she cannily, deliberately, takes upon herself (though with a handsome young fellow like Orlando wandering about the forest scratching "Ros-

alind" on every tree there is nothing that would please her more than
to be revealed) and in the "South-sea of discovery" it allows her to
make. For if Orlando discovers culture—sonnets and banquets—in the
forest, Rosalind discovers nature, and rejoices in the occasion for the
expression of her own ebullient, versatile and polymorph energies. It is
a superbly audacious idea, this saucy lackey cure for love, if she can
bring it off:

> At which time would I, being but a moonish youth, grieve,
> be effeminate, changeable, longing and liking, proud, fan-
> tastical, apish, shallow, inconstant, full of tears, full of smiles;
> for every passion something, and for no passion truly any
> thing, as boys and women are for the most part cattle of this
> color; would now like him, now loathe him; then entertain
> him, then forswear him; now weep for him, then spit at
> him; . . . and this way will I take upon me to wash your
> liver as clean as a sound sheep's heart, that there shall not be
> one spot of love in't.
>
> (3.2.409–24)

And if she can bring it off, how can she lose? She is invisible. She is in
control. She is master-mistress of the situation. She can discover not
only what he is like, but what she is like; test his feelings, test her own;
mock love and mask love and make love; provoke and bask in the
attentions of the lover whose company she most desires, pretend to be
the boy she always wanted, perhaps, to be, and permit herself extrava-
gances everyday decorum would certainly preclude: "Come, woo me,
woo me; for now I am in a holiday humor, and like enough to
consent. What would you say to me now, and I were your very very
Rosalind?" (4.1.68–71).

It is no wonder the gaiety of this twinned character is infectious,
the ebullience irrepressible, the high spirits inimitable. She / he
is all things to all men and enjoys every moment of this androgynous
ventriloquist's carnival, the more especially since, unlike her sisters
in disguise, Julia and Viola, she has the relief of candid self-exposure
to her confidante Celia as well: "O coz, coz, coz, my pretty little
coz, that thou didst know how many fathom deep I am in love!
But it cannot be sounded; my affection hath an unknown bottom,
like the bay of Portugal" (4.1.205–8). "You have simply misus'd
our sex in your love-prate," complains the soberer Celia, concerned for sexual solidarity. But what is sexual solidarity to her is

to her chameleon cousin sexual solipsism and she will have none of it.

She provokes preposterously, and so exorcizes (in this a double for Orlando) the paranoia of male anti-feminism with her dire threat:

> I will be more jealous of thee than a Barbary cock-pigeon over his hen, more clamorous than a parrot against rain, more new-fangled than an ape, more giddy in my desires than a monkey. I will weep for nothing, like Diana in the fountain, and I will do that when you are disposed to be merry. I will laugh like a hyen, and that when you are inclin'd to sleep.
>
> (4.1.149–56)

only to reveal herself with utter if inadvertent candour the next moment: "Alas, dear love, I cannot lack thee two hours" (4.1.178) and then, to cover her slip, immediately dissimulates again in the mock tirade of an abused and long-suffering wife: "Ay, go your ways, go your ways; I knew what you would prove; my friends told me as much, and I thought no less. That flattering tongue of yours won me. 'Tis but one cast away, and so come death! Two a'clock is your hour?" (4.1.185–86).

Her double role is a triumph of characterization through impersonation, inconsistency, not consistency, being the key to dramatic verisimilitude if a complex and dynamic individual is to be represented. More, Rosalind, the girl, in whom natural impulse is finely cultivated and worldly wisdom cohabits with a passionate nature, together with her own "twin" Ganymede, in whom a youth's beauty and a youth's jaunty irreverence combine, provides the double indemnity of comedy with lavish generosity. The duality of her masculine and feminine roles—itself an abolition of disjunction—gratifies our craving both for pleasure and reality, satisfies a deep defensive need for intellectual scepticism as well as an equally deep need for impulsive and limitless abandon, provides at once for cerebration and celebration, resolves the dichotomies of nature and culture, wisdom and folly, mockery and festivity.

I find in a recent study of what existential psychologists call "peak experience," interesting confirmation of the theory of comic therapy Shakespeare's practice, particularly in this play, appears to support. "Peak experiences," says Abraham H. Maslow, make characters in plays and their audiences more apt to feel "that life in general is worth while, even if it is usually drab, pedestrian, painful or ungratifying, since beauty, excitement, honesty, play, goodness, truth, and meaningfulness have been demonstrated to him to exist. . . . Life itself is validated, and suicide and death wishing must become less likely." [*Towards a Psychology of Being*].

Thus the make-believe courtship, invented on the pretext of furnishing a cure for Orlando's love melancholy (or at least for his versification!), provides Rosalind with a homeopathic *remedia amoris* for hers. Free to fantasize, explore, experiment, she confers upon the audience a vivid sense that the mortal coil might not be solely a curse, nor the working-day world of briars beyond transfiguring.

And even that is not all. Ganymede's undertaking to cure Orlando's love-longing passes the time entertainingly in the greenwood but it also runs Rosalind into difficulties with the native population, thus providing the canonical knot of errors through a mistaken identity, and Ganymede with more livers to wash as clean as a sound sheep's heart.

Phebe's high-handed scorn for her doleful lover's courtly style exposes the substance of her own callousness as well as the absurd affectations of courtly love:

> 'Tis pretty, sure, and very probable,
> That eyes, that are the frail'st and softest things,
> Who shut their coward gates on atomies,
> Should be called tyrants, butchers, murtherers!
> Now I do frown on thee with all my heart,
> And if mine eyes can wound, now let them kill thee.
> Now counterfeit to swound; why, now fall down,
> Or if thou canst not, O, for shame, for shame,
> Lie not, to say mine eyes are murtherers!
>
> (3.5.11–19)

Rosalind, too, knows that "these are all lies"; that "men have died from time to time, and worms have eaten them, but not for love" (4.1.108), she, too, knows that "men are April when they woo, December when they wed," and that maids "are May when they are maids, but the sky changes when they are wives" (4.1.147–48). But her realism is of another order altogether than Phebe's callow literalism, and is vouched for by the vigour with which she scolds the pair of them, combining the swashbuckling gusto of Ganymede with the passionate sincerity of Rosalind, in a *nosce teipsum* totally free of illusion:

'Od's my little life,
I think she means to tangle my eyes too!
No, faith, proud mistress, hope not after it.
'Tis not your inky brows, your black silk hair,
Your bugle eyeballs, nor your cheek of cream
That can entame my spirits to your worship.
You foolish shepherd, wherefore do you follow her,
Like foggy south, puffing with wind and rain?
You are a thousand times a properer man
Than she a woman. 'Tis such fools as you
That make the world full of ill-favor'd children.
'Tis not her glass, but you that flatters her,
And out of you she sees her self more proper
Than any of her lineaments can show her.
But, mistress, know yourself, down on your knees,
And thank heaven, fasting, for a good man's love;
For I must tell you friendly in your ear,
Sell when you can, you are not for all markets.

(3.5.43–60)

Ralph Berry takes a counterview of *As You Like It*, and especially
of this incident. He finds unease, irritation and hostility—the groundswell
of a power struggle latent or overt—to be the dominant motif of the
play. This, however, is a view as overselective as Jaques's seven ages
speech. What is leaves out is the fun. But it is also not strictly accurate.
Berry accounts, for instance, for the "quite astonishing warmth" of
Rosalind's diatribe—"thirty odd lines of vulgar abuse" he calls it—in
terms of Phebe appearing to Rosalind as a subtly threatening parallel or
caricature of herself. "Phebe is a domineering woman who . . . has
mastered her man; so is Rosalind." But when the incident occurs
Rosalind has mastered no one. She has merely suggested to Orlando
that they meet again. Phebe is, to be sure, the phantom Ganymede
conjures to cure Orlando of just such love-longing as Silvius's. The
caricature double surely provides a foil to the hidden Rosalind; and the
comedy arising from the idea of Rosalind meeting a "real" embodi-
ment of Ganymede's fantasy is quite lost in Berry's reductive reading.

It is no wonder that Phebe, whose dejected lover Silvius is clearly
not manly enough for his imperious mistress, falls head over heels in
love with this high-spirited outspokenness, thus hoisting Rosalind /
Ganymede with his / her own epicene petard. Ganymede has in his

face that which Phebe would feign call master, it seems, and this is a tangle not easy to untie. A remedy for deadlock, however, is provided by the very occurrence which virtually exhausts the Ganymede device. The arrival of Oliver, reformed by his experience of courtly treachery, with the tale of his brother's heroic rescue (a recapitulation of the native *virtu* of the wrestling exploit on a higher moral level) provides not only proof that Orlando is no tame snake like Silvius, but also a patrimony for him and a partner for Celia. The exhaustion of the comic device is neatly dramatized by the emotional collapse of Rosalind at the sight of the bloodied handkerchief, and there is now nothing in the world to prevent the trickster heroine from undoing the turmoil she has caused. Her power to do this is beautifully "masqued" by the chiming quarter of act 5, scene 2: Love is "to be made of sighs and tears"—

> SILVIUS: And so am I for Phebe.
> PHEBE: And I for Ganymede.
> ORLANDO: And I for Rosalind.
> ROSALIND: And I for no woman
>
> (5.2.85–93)

and so on, until Rosalind begs, "Pray you no more of this, 'tis like the howling of Irish wolves against the moon" (5.2.109–10).

This is the ironic voice which ends the play with the classic plea for applause in the epilogue, and it is worth a moment's further reflection. That Rosalind is still dressed as Ganymede has been convincingly argued in terms of the scarcity of time available at that point for a boy to change into elaborate women's clothing. But there is a cogent argument to be drawn from the play's own dialectical resolution. If she is still Ganymede in the epilogue, then "If I were a woman" is spoken out of her saucy lackey role, as the man-of-the-world bawdy of "that between you and the women the play may please" seems to suggest. She is thus drawing the audience, too, into her transvestite trickster's net, prolonging the duplicity of self-discovery and self-concealment, the enchanting game of both / and. But if she is dressed as Rosalind, then "If I were a woman" is spoken over the heads, so to speak, of characters and play, by the boy-actor of Shakespeare's company, and this will *collapse* the dramatic illusion of "real" make-believe from which the whole play draws its dynamic power. Shakespeare, I submit, is not calling attention to his play as play, as opposed to reality: he is calling attention to Rosalind's "play" as a component reality would do well to absorb.

At the end of *As You Like It* dukes are restored to their dukedoms, sons to their inheritances. Wickedness has burst, like a boil, by some mysterious spontaneous combustion, leaving not a rack behind. But not all Jacks have their Jills. Jaques is unassimilated. But he is by nature a solitary and continues his travels, happily sucking melancholy out of all occasions as a weasel sucks eggs, on the outer edge of remedy.

There is also unaccommodated William at the marriage feast. But there's hope even there, if Touchstone's fidelity can be relied upon; Jaques gives him two months (5.4.192). For though "wedlock," in the view of that philosopher of life's most minimal expectations, "will be nibbling," what of it?

> But what though? Courage! As horns are odious, they are necessary. It is said, 'Many a man knows no end of his goods'. Right! many a man has good horns and knows no end of them. Well, that is the dowry of his wife, 'tis none of his own getting. Horns? even so. Poor men alone? No, no, the noblest deer hath them as huge as the rascal. Is the single man therefore bless'd? No, as a wall'd town is more worthier than a village, so is the forehead of a married man more honorable than the bare brow of a bachelor.
>
> (3.3.51–61)

If this is a mockery of "romance" it is also a mockery of "reason." A protuberance is a protuberance, whether it be the bastion of a walled town or the horned frontlet of a married man. To Touchstone, logic is a bagatelle. All is immaterially interchangeable: court and country, culture and nature, fact and fiction, sense and folly, wedlock and non-wedlock, for that matter, too. Earthly things made even atone together in Touchstone's anti-logic as well as in Hymen's conjuration. Touchstone's courtship has been a mocking parody of the affectations of the mid-level characters Phebe and Silvius; but he is also a mocking foil to Rosalind's superior synthesis of culture and nature, just as his bawdy "prick" song (If a hart do lack a hind [3.2.100–112]) is foil to her own frank naturalism. In this matter she can give as good as she gets, too, in Mercutio's very vein (3.2.117–20).

"Rosalind, Viola, and, to a less extent Beatrice," says Charlton, (forgetting, however, Julia and Hippolyta), have entered into the possession of spiritual endowments which, if hitherto suspected to exist at all, had either been distrusted as dangerous or had become moribund through desuetude . . . they have claimed the intuitive, the subconscious, and the emotional as instruments by which personality may bring itself to a fuller consciousness of and a completer harmony with the realities of existence. They have left Theseus far behind; they have also outgrown Falstaff.

[H. B. Charlton, *Shakespearean Comedy*]

It is perhaps, as I have tried to show, less a matter of outgrowing Falstaff, then of replacing him, by a new combination: the Lady and the Fool. Touchstone is a professional jester, not a bumbling village constable or a Bacchic life-force. He is not a merry fool, either. He is too Ecclesiastes-wise; and besides his feet hurt. But his burlesque fool's wisdom serves throughout most excellently to mediate our recognition of the Erastian higher folly of his ebullient mistress. When Wylie Sypher speaks, [in *Comedy*], of "the unruliness of the flesh and its vitality," he characterizes the buffoon nature in all its manifestations. "Comedy," Sypher continues, "is essentially a carrying away of Death, a triumph over mortality by some absurd faith in rebirth, restoration, salvation." Perhaps we could say that Touchstone epitomizes the absurdity, and Rosalind the faith; and that it is the interlocking and paradoxical partnership of the two that characterizes this second, and second last of Shakespeare's post-Falstaffian comedies.

Shakespeare is not done with the wayward and unruly erotic passions. Nor will he be, needless to say, until the last word he contributes to *Two Noble Kinsmen*. But his romantic comedy treatment of them does come to an end with his next play *Twelfth Night*, in which the rivalries and duplicities, twinnings and doublings of the battle of the sexes are further extended into the ambivalent twinnings, duplicities and doublings within the lovers' own individual identities.

"The Place of a Brother" in *As You Like It:* Social Process and Comic Form

Louis Adrian Montrose

As You Like It creates and resolves conflict by mixing what the characters call Fortune and Nature—the circumstances in which they find
themselves, as opposed to the resources of playfulness and boldness,
moral virtue and witty deception, with which they master adversity
and fulfill their desires.

The romantic action is centered on the meeting, courtship, and
successful pairing of Rosalind and Orlando. This action is complicated,
as Leo Salingar reminds us, by "a cardinal social assumption . . .
(which would have been obvious to . . . Shakespeare's first audiences)
—that Rosalind is a princess, while Orlando is no more than a gentleman. But for the misfortune of her father's exile, they might not have
met in sympathy as at first; but for the second misfortune of her own
exile, as well as his, they could not have met in apparent equality in the
Forest." The personal situations of Rosalind and Orlando affect, and
are affected by, their relationship to each other. Rosalind's union with
Orlando entails the weakening of her ties to her natural father and to a
cousin who has been closer to her than a sister; Orlando's union with
Rosalind entails the strengthening of his ties to his elder brother and to
a lord who becomes his patron. Orlando's atonements with other
men—a natural brother, a social father—precede his atonement with
Rosalind. They confirm that the disadvantaged young country gentleman is worthy of the princess, by "nature" and by "fortune." The

From *Shakespeare Quarterly* 32, no. 1 (Spring 1981). © 1981 by the Folger Shakespeare
Library.

atonement of earthly things celebrated in Hymen's wedding song incorporates man and woman within a process that reunites man with man. This process is my subject.

As the play begins, Orlando and Adam are discussing the terms of a paternal will; the first scene quickly explodes into fraternal resentment and envy, hatred and violence. By the end of the second scene, the impoverished youngest son of Sir Rowland de Boys finds himself victimized by "a tyrant Duke" and "a tyrant brother" (1.3.278). The compact early scenes expose hostilities on the manor and in the court that threaten to destroy both the family and the state. Although modern productions have shown that these scenes can be powerful and effective in the theatre, modern criticism has repeatedly downplayed their seriousness and significance. They are often treated merely as Shakespeare's mechanism for propelling his characters—and us—into the forest as quickly and efficiently as possible. Thus Harold Jenkins, in his influential essay on the play, writes of "the inconsequential nature of the action" and of "Shakespeare's haste to get ahead"; for him, the plot's interest consists in Shakespeare's ability to get "most of it over in the first act." If we *reverse* Jenkins's perspective, we will do justice to Shakespeare's dramaturgy and make better sense of the play. What happens to Orlando at home is not Shakespeare's contrivance to get him into the forest; what happens to Orlando in the forest is Shakespeare's contrivance to remedy what has happened to him at home. The form of *As You Like It* becomes comic in the process of resolving the conflicts that are generated within it; events unfold and relationships are transformed in accordance with a precise comic teleology.

II

Jaques sententiously observes that the world is a stage; the men and women, merely players; and one man's time, a sequence of acts in which he plays many parts. Shakespeare's plays reveal many traces of the older drama's intimate connection to the annual agrarian and ecclesiastical cycles. But more pervasive than these are the connections between Shakespearean comic and tragic forms and the human life cycle—the sequence of acts performed in several ages by Jaques's social player. Action in Shakespearean drama usually originates in combinations of a few basic kinds of human conflict: conflict among members of different families, generations, sexes, and social classes. Shakespeare tends to focus dramatic action precisely *between* the social "acts," between the sequential "ages," in the fictional lives of his characters. Many of the plays turn upon points of transition in the life cycle— birth, puberty, marriage, death—where discontinuities arise and where adjustments are necessary to basic interrelationships in the family and in society. Such dramatic actions are analogous to rites of passage. Transition rites symbolically impose markers upon the life cycle and safely conduct people from one stage of life to the next; they give a social shape, order, and sanction to personal existence.

In *As You Like It*, the initial conflict arises from the circumstances of inheritance by primogeniture. The differential relationship between the first born and his younger brothers is profoundly augmented at their father's death: the eldest son assumes a paternal relationship to his siblings; and the potential for sibling conflict increases when the relationship between brother and brother becomes identified with the relationship between father and son. The transition of the father from life to death both fosters and obstructs the transition of his sons from childhood to manhood. In *As You Like It*, the process of comedy accomplishes successful passages between ages in the life cycle and ranks in the social hierarchy. By the end of the play, Orlando has been brought from an impoverished and powerless adolescence to the threshold of manhood and marriage, wealth and title.

A social anthropologist defines inheritance practices as "the way by which property is transmitted between the living and the dead, and especially between generations."

> Inheritance is not only the means by which the reproduction of the social system is carried out . . . it is also the way in which interpersonal relationships are structured. . . .
>
> The linking of patterns of inheritance with patterns of domestic organization is a matter not simply of numbers and formations but of attitudes and emotions. The manner of splitting property is a manner of splitting people; it creates (or in some cases reflects) a particular constellation of ties and cleavages between husband and wife, parents and children, sibling and sibling, as well as between wider kin.
>
> [Jack Goody, "Introduction," in *Family and Inheritance: Rural Society in Western Europe, 1200–1800,* ed. Jack Goody, Joan Thirsk, and E. P. Thompson]

As Goody himself concedes, the politics of the family are most powerfully anatomized, not by historians or social scientists, but by playwrights. Parents and children in Shakespeare's plays are recurrently giving or withholding, receiving or returning, property and love. Material and spiritual motives, self-interest and self-sacrifice, are inextricably intertwined in Shakespearean drama as in life.

Lear's tragedy, for example, begins in his division of his kingdom among his daughters and their husbands. He makes a bequest of his property to his heirs before his death, so "that future strife / May be prevented now" (1.1.44–45). Gloucester's tragedy begins in the act of adultery that begets an "unpossessing bastard" (2.1.67). Edmund rails against "the plague of custom . . . the curiosity of nations" (1.2.3–4); he sees himself as victimized by rules of legitimacy and primogeniture. *As You Like It* begins with Orlando remembering the poor bequest from a dead father and the unnaturalness of an elder brother; he is victimized by what he bitterly refers to as "the courtesy of nations" (1.1.45–46). Rosalind dejectedly remembers "a banished father" (1.2.4) and the consequent loss of her own preeminent social place. Celia responds to her cousin with naive girlhood loyalty: "You know my father hath no child but I, nor none is like to have; and truly when he dies, thou shalt be his heir; for what he hath taken away from thy father perforce, I will render thee again in affection" (1.2.14–19). The comic action of *As You Like It* works to atone elder and younger brothers, father and child, man and woman, lord and subject, master and servant. Within his play, Rosalind's magician-uncle recreates situations that are recurrent sources of ambiguity, anxiety, and conflict in the society of his audience; he explores and exacerbates them, and he resolves them by brilliant acts of theatrical prestidigitation.

The tense situation which begins *As You Like It* was a familiar and controversial fact of Elizabethan social life. Lawrence Stone emphasizes that "the prime factor affecting all families which owned property was . . . primogeniture"; that "the principle and practice of primogeniture . . . went far to determine the behaviour and character of both parents and children, and to govern the relationship between siblings" [*The Family, Sex and Marriage in England 1500–1800*]. In the sixteenth and seventeenth centuries, primogeniture was more widely and rigorously practiced in England—by the gentry and lesser landowners, as well as by the aristocracy—than anywhere else in Europe. The consequent hardships, frequent abuses, and inherent inequities of primogeniture generated a "literature of protest by and for younger sons" that has been characterized as "plentiful," "vehement" in tone, and "unanimous" in its sympathies [Joan Thirsk, "Younger Sons in the Seventeenth Century," *History* (London), 54 (1969)].

Jaques was not the only satirist to "rail against all the first-born of Egypt" (2.5.57–58). John Earle included the character of a "younger Brother" in his *Micro-Cosmographie* (1628):

> His father ha's done with him, as *Pharaoh* to the children of Israel, that would have them make brick, and give them no straw, so he taskes him to bee a Gentleman, and leaves him nothing to maintaine it. The pride of his house has undone him, which the elder Knighthood must sustaine, and his beggery that Knighthood. His birth and bringing up will not suffer him to descend to the meanes to get wealth: but hee stands at the mercy of the world, and which is worse of his brother. He is something better then the Servingmen; yet they more saucy with him, then hee bold with the master, who beholds him with a countenance of sterne awe, and checks him oftner then his Liveries. . . . Nature hath furnisht him with a little more wit upon compassion; for it is like to be his best revenew. . . . Hee is commonly discontented, and desperate, and the forme of his exclamation is, that Churle my brother.

As a class, the gentry experienced a relative rise in wealth and status during this period. But the rise was achieved by inheriting eldest sons at the expense of their younger brothers. As Earle and other contemporaries clearly recognized, the gentry's drive to aggrandize and perpetuate their estates led them to a ruthless application of primogeniture; this left them without the means adequately to provide for their other offspring. The psychological and socioeconomic consequences of primogeniture for younger sons (and for daughters) seem to have been considerable: downward social mobility and relative impoverishment, inability to marry or late marriage, and fewer children.

In 1600, about the time *As You Like It* was first performed, Thomas Wilson wrote a valuable analysis of England's social structure. His description of gentlemen reveals a very personal involvement:

> Those which wee call Esquires are gentlemen whose ancestors are or have bin Knights, or else they are the heyres and eldest of their houses and of some competent quantity of revenue fitt to be called to office and authority in their Country. . . . These are the elder brothers.

> I cannot speak of the number of yonger brothers, albeit I
> be one of the number myselfe, but for their estate there is no
> man hath better cause to knowe it, nor less cause to praise it;
> their state is of all stations for gentlemen most misera-
> ble. . . . [A father] may demise as much as he thinkes good
> to his younger children, but such a fever hectick hath custome
> brought in and inured amongst fathers, and such fond desire
> they have to leave a great shewe of the stock of their house,
> though the branches be withered, that they will not doe it,
> but my elder brother forsooth must be my master. He must
> have all, and all the rest that which the catt left on the malt
> heape, perhaps some smale annuytye during his life or what
> please our elder brother's worship to bestowe upon us if
> wee please him.

The foregoing texts characterize quite precisely the situation of Orlando and his relationship to Oliver at the beginning of *As You Like It.*
They suggest that Shakespeare's audience may have responded with
some intensity to Orlando's indictment of "the courtesy of nations."

In his constitutional treatise, *De Republica Anglorum* (written ca.
1562; printed 1583), Sir Thomas Smith observes that "whosoever
studies the laws of the realm, who studies at the universities, who
professes liberal sciences and to be short, who can live idly and without manual labour, and will bear the port, charge and countenance of a
gentleman . . . shall be taken for a gentleman." The expected social
fate of a gentleborn Elizabethan younger son was to lose the ease founded
upon landed wealth that was the very hallmark of gentility. Joan Thirsk
suggests that, although there were places to be had for those who were
industrious and determined to make the best of their misfortune,

> the habit of working for a living was not ingrained in
> younger sons of this class, and no amount of argument
> could convince them of the justice of treating them so differ-
> ently from their elder brothers. The contrast was too sharp
> between the life of an elder son, whose fortune was made
> for him by his father, and who had nothing to do but
> maintain, and perhaps augment it, and that of the younger
> sons who faced a life of hard and continuous effort, starting
> almost from nothing. Many persistently refused to accept
> their lot, and hung around at home, idle, bored, and increas-
> ingly resentful.

At the beginning of *As You Like It,* Orlando accuses Oliver of enforcing his idleness and denying him the means to preserve the gentility which is his birthright: "My brother Jaques he keeps at school, and report speaks goldenly of his profit; for my part, he keeps me rustically at home, or, to speak more properly, stays me here at home unkept; for call you that keeping for a gentleman of my birth, that differs not from the stalling of an ox? . . . [He] mines my gentility with my education" (1.1.5–10, 20–21). Orlando is "not taught to make anything" (1.1.30); and his natural virtue is marred "with idleness" (1.2.33–34). When Adam urges him to leave the family estate, Orlando imagines his only prospects to be beggary and highway robbery (2.3.29–34). He finally agrees to go off with Adam, spending the old laborer's "youthful wages" in order to gain "some settled low content" (2.3.67–68).

Shakespeare's opening strategy is to plunge his characters and his audience into the controversy about a structural principle of Elizabethan personal, family, and social life. He is not merely using something topical to get his comedy off to a lively start: the expression and resolution of sibling conflict and its social implications are integral to the play's form and function. The process of comedy works against the seemingly inevitable prospect of social degradation suggested at the play's beginning, and against its literary idealization in conventions of humble pastoral retirement. In the course of *As You Like It,* Orlando's gentility is preserved and his material well-being is enhanced. Shakespeare uses the machinery of pastoral romance to remedy the lack of fit between deserving and having, between Nature and Fortune. Without actually violating the primary Elizabethan social frontier separating the gentle from the base, the play achieves an illusion of social leveling and of unions across class boundaries. Thus, people of every rank in Shakespeare's socially heterogeneous audience might construe the action as they liked it.

Primogeniture is rarely mentioned in modern commentaries on *As You Like It,* despite its obvious prominence in the text and in the action. Shakespeare's treatment of primogeniture may very well have been a vital—perhaps even the dominant—source of engagement for many in his Elizabethan audience. The public theatre brought together people from all the status and occupational groups to be found in Shakespeare's London (except, of course, for the poorest laborers and the indigent). Alfred Harbage points out that the two groups "mentioned again and again in contemporary allusions to the theatres" are "the students of the Inns of Court and the apprentices of London." In addition to these youthful groups, significant numbers of soldiers, professionals, merchants, shopkeepers, artisans, and household servants were also regular playgoers. The careers most available to the younger sons of gentlemen were in the professions—most notably the law, but also medicine and teaching—as well as in trade, the army, and the church. Thus, Shakespeare's audience must have included a high proportion of gentleborn younger sons—adults, as well as the youths who were students and apprentices. Among these gentleborn younger sons, and among the baseborn youths who were themselves socially subordinate apprentices and servants, it is likely that Orlando's desperate situation was the focus of personal projections and a catalyst of powerful feelings. "During the sixteenth century," Thirsk concludes, "to describe anyone as 'a younger son' was a short-hand way of summing up a host of grievances. . . . Younger son meant an angry young man, bearing more than his share of injustice and resentment, deprived of means by his father and elder brother, often hanging around his elder brother's house as a servant, completely dependent on his grace and favour." Youths, younger sons, and all Elizabethan playgoers who felt that Fortune's benefits had been "mightily misplaced" (2.1.33–34) could identify with Shakespeare's Orlando.

III

It is precisely in the details of inheritance that Shakespeare makes one of the most significant departures from his source. Sir John of Bordeaux is on his deathbed at the beginning of Lodge's *Rosalynde*; he divides his land and chattels among his three sons:

> Unto thee *Saladyne* the eldest, and therefore the chiefest piller of my house, wherein should be ingraven as well the excellence of thy fathers qualities, as the essentiall forme of his proportion, to thee I give fourteene ploughlands, with all my Mannor houses and richest plate. Next unto *Fernadyne* I bequeath twelve ploughlands. But unto *Rosader* the youngest I give my Horse, my Armour and my Launce, with sixteene ploughlands: for if inward thoughts be discovered by outward shadowes, *Rosader* will exceed you all in bountie and honour.

The partible inheritance devised by Lodge's Sir John was an idiosyncratic variation on practices widespread in Elizabethan society among those outside the gentry. Saladyne, the eldest born, inherits his father's authority. Rosader receives more land and love—he is his father's joy, although his last and least. Saladyne, who becomes Rosader's guardian, is deeply resentful and decides not to honor their father's will: "What man thy Father is dead, and hee can neither helpe thy fortunes, nor measure thy actions: therefore, burie his words with his carkasse, and bee wise for thy selfe."

Lodge's text, like Thomas Wilson's, reminds us that primogeniture was not a binding law but rather a flexible social custom in which the propertied sought to perpetuate themselves by preserving their estates intact through successive generations. Shakespeare alters the terms of the paternal will in Lodge's story so as to alienate Orlando from the status of a landed gentleman. The effect is to intensify the differences between the eldest son and his siblings, and to identify the sibling conflict with the major division in the Elizabethan social fabric: that between the landed and the unlanded, the gentle and the base. (Within half a century after Shakespeare wrote *As You Like It,* radical pamphleteers were using "elder brother" and "younger brother" as synonyms for the propertied, enfranchised social classes and the unpropertied, unenfranchised social classes.) Primogeniture complicates not only sibling and socioeconomic relationships but also relationships between generations: between a father and the eldest son impatient for his inheritance; between a father and the younger sons resentful against the "fever hectic" that custom has inured among fathers.

Shakespeare's plays are thickly populated by subjects, sons, and younger brothers who are ambivalently bound to their lords, genitors, and elder siblings—and by young women moving ambivalently between the lordships of father and husband. If this dramatic proliferation of patriarchs suggests that Shakespeare had a neurotic obsession, then it was one with a social context. To see father-figures everywhere in Shakespeare's plays is not a psychoanalytic anachronism, for Shakespeare's own contemporaries seem to have seen father-figures everywhere. The period from the mid-sixteenth to the mid-seventeenth century in England has been characterized by Lawrence Stone as "the patriarchal stage in the evolution of the nuclear family." Writing of the early seventeenth-century family as "a political symbol and a social institution," Gordon J. Schochet documents that

> virtually all social relationships—not merely those between
> fathers and children and magistrates and subjects—were re-

garded as patriarchal or familial in essence. The family was looked upon as the basis of the entire social order. . . .

So long as a person occupied an inferior status within a household—as a child, servant, apprentice, or even as a wife—and was subordinated to the head, his social identity was altogether vicarious. . . .

Before a man achieved social status—if he ever did—he would have spent a great many years in various positions of patriarchal subordination.

[*Patriarchalism in Political Thought*]

This social context shaped Shakespeare's preoccupation with fathers; and it gave him the scope within which to reshape it into drama, satisfying his own needs and those of his paying audience. His plays explore the difficulty or impossibility of establishing or authenticating a self in a rigorously hierarchical and patriarchal society, a society in which full social identity tends to be limited to propertied adult males who are the heads of households.

Shakespeare's Sir Rowland de Boys is dead before the play begins. But the father endures in the power exerted by his memory and his will upon the men in the play—his sons, Adam, the dukes—and upon their attitudes toward each other. The play's very first words insinuate that Orlando's filial feeling is ambivalent "As I remember, Adam, it was upon this fashion bequeathed me by will but poor a thousand crowns, and, as thou sayst, charged my brother on his blessing to breed me well; and there begins my sadness" (1.1.1–4). Orlando's diction is curiously indirect; he conspicuously avoids naming his father. Absent from Shakespeare's play is any expression of the special, compensatory paternal affection shown to Lodge's Rosader. There is an implied resentment against an unnamed father, who has left his son a paltry inheritance and committed him to an indefinite and socially degrading dependence upon his own brother. Ironically, Orlando's first explicit acknowledgment of his filial bond is in a declaration of personal *independence,* a repudiation of his bondage to his eldest brother: "The spirit of my father, which I think is within me, begins to mutiny against this servitude" (1.1.21–23). Orlando's assertions of filial piety are actually self-assertions, directed against his father's eldest son. As Sir Rowland's inheritor, Oliver perpetuates Orlando's subordination within the patriarchal order; he usurps Orlando's selfhood.

In a private family and household, the eldest son succeeds the father as patriarch. In a royal or aristocratic family, the eldest son also succeeds to the father's title and political authority. Thus, when he has been crowned as King Henry V, Hal tells his uneasy siblings, "I'll be your father and your brother too. / Let me but bear your love, I'll bear your cares" (*2 Henry IV,* 5.2.57–58). Like Henry, Oliver is simultaneously a father and a brother to his own natural sibling; he is at once Orlando's master and his peer. Primogeniture conflates the generations in the person of the elder brother and blocks the generational passage of the younger brother. What might be described dispassionately as a contradiction in social categories is incarnated in the play, as in English social life, in family conflicts and identity crises.

Orlando gives bitter expression to his personal experience of this social contradiction: "The courtesy of nations allows you my better in that you are the firstborn, but that same tradition takes not away my blood, were there twenty brothers betwixt us. I have as much of my father in me as you, albeit I confess that your coming before me is nearer his reverence" (1.1.45–51). Here Orlando asserts that all brothers are equally their father's sons. Oliver might claim a special paternal relationship because he is the first born; but Orlando's own claim actually to incorporate their father renders insubstantial any argument based on age or birth order. Thus, Orlando can indict his brother and repudiate his authority: "You have trained me like a peasant, obscuring and hiding from me all gentlemanlike qualities. The spirit of my father grows strong in me, and I will no longer endure it" (1.1.68–71). Because the patriarchal family is the basic political unit of a patriarchal society, Orlando's protests suggest that primogeniture involves contradictions in the categories of social status as well as those of kinship. Orlando is subordinated to his sibling as a son to his father; and he is subordinated to a fellow gentleman as a peasant would be subordinated to his lord.

Orlando incorporates not only his father's likeness and name ("Rowland") but also his potent "spirit"—his personal genius, his manliness, and his moral virtue. To Adam, Orlando is "gentle, strong, and valiant" (2.3.6). He is his father's gracious and virtuous reincarnation: "O you memory of old Sir Rowland!" (2.3.3–4). Adam challenges the eldest son's legal claim to be his father's heir by asserting that Oliver is morally undeserving, that he is *spiritually* illegitimate:

> Your brother, no, no brother, yet the son—
> Yet not the son, I will not call him son—

> Of him I was about to call his father.
> (2.3.19–21)

Orlando's claim to his spiritual inheritance leads immediately to physical coercion: Oliver calls him "boy" and strikes him. Orlando responds to this humiliating form of paternal chastisement not with deference but with rebellion: he puts his hands to Oliver's throat. Orlando's assertion of a self which "remembers" their father is a threat to Oliver's patriarchal authority, a threat to his own social identity: "Begin you to grow upon me?" (1.1.85). The brothers' natural bond, in short, is contaminated by their ambiguous social relationship.

Because fraternity is confused with filiation—because the generations have, in effect, been collapsed together—the conflict of elder and younger brothers also projects an oedipal struggle between father and son. In the second scene, the private violence between the brothers is displaced into the public wrestling match. Oliver tells Charles, the Duke's wrestler, "I had as lief thou didst break [Orlando's] neck as his finger" (1.1.144–45). Sinewy Charles, the "general challenger" (1.2.159), has already broken the bodies of "three proper young men" (1.1.111) before Orlando comes in to try "the strength of [his] youth" (1.1.161). In a sensational piece of stage business, Orlando and Charles enact a living emblem of the generational struggle. When Orlando throws Charles, youth is supplanting age, the son is supplanting the father. This contest is preceded by a remarkable exchange:

> CHARLES: Come, where is this young gallant that is so
>   desirous to lie with his mother earth?
> ORLANDO: Ready sir, but his will hath in it a more modest
>   working.
>
> (1.2.188–91)

Charles's challenge gives simultaneous expression to a filial threat of incest and a paternal threat of filicide. In this conspicuously motherless play, the social context of reciprocal father-son hostility is a male struggle for identity and power fought between elders and youths, first-born and younger brothers.

Orlando's witty response to Charles suggests that he regards neither his fears nor his threats. Orlando's "will" is merely to come to man's estate and to preserve the status of a gentleman. At the beginning of *As You Like It,* then, Shakespeare sets himself the problem of resolving the consequences of a conflict between Orlando's powerful assertion of identity—his spiritual claim to be a true inheritor—and the social fact that he is a subordinated and disadvantaged younger son. In the forest, Oliver will be spiritually reborn and confirmed in his original inheritance. Orlando will be socially reborn as heir apparent to the reinstated Duke. Orlando will regain a brother by "blood" and a father by "affinity."

IV

Orlando is not only a younger son but also a youth. And in its language, characterization, and plot, As You Like It emphasizes the significance of age categories. Most prominent, of course, is Jaques's disquisition on the seven ages of man. But the play's *dramatis personae* actually fall into the three functional age groups of Elizabethan society: youth, maturity, and old age. Orlando's youth is referred to by himself and by others some two dozen times in the first two scenes: he is young; a boy; a youth; the youngest son; a younger brother; a young fellow; a young gallant; a young man; a young gentleman. Social historians have discredited the notion that adolescence went unexperienced or unacknowledged in early modern England. Lawrence Stone, for example, emphasizes that in Shakespeare's time there was "a strong contemporary consciousness of adolescence (then called 'youth'), as a distinct stage of life between sexual maturity at about fifteen and marriage at about twenty-six." Shakespeare's persistent epithets identify Orlando as a member of the group about which contemporary moralists and guardians of the social order were most obsessively concerned. The Statute of Artificers (1563) summarizes the official attitude: "Until a man grow unto the age of twenty-four years he . . . is wild, without judgment and not of sufficient experience to govern himself." The youthful members of an Elizabethan household—children, servants, and apprentices—were all supposed to be kept under strict patriarchal control. Stone points out that "it was precisely because its junior members were under close supervision that the state had a very strong interest in encouraging and strengthening the household. . . . It helped to keep in check potentially the most unruly element in any society, the floating mass of young unmarried males." Orlando is physically mature and powerful, but socially infantilized and weak.

That Shakespeare should focus so many of his plays on a sympathetic consideration of the problems of youth is not surprising when we consider that perhaps half the population was under twenty, and that the youthfulness of Shakespeare's society was reflected in the composition of his audience. In his richly documented study ["Age and Authority"], Keith Thomas demonstrates that

> So far as the young were concerned, the sixteenth and seventeenth centuries are conspicuous for a sustained drive to subordinate persons in their teens and early twenties and to delay their equal participation in the adult world. This drive is reflected in the wider dissemination of apprenticeship; in the involvement of many more children in formal education; and in a variety of measures to prolong the period of legal and social infancy.

Elizabethan adolescence seems to have been characterized by a high degree of geographical mobility: youths were sent off to school, to search for work as living-in servants, or to be apprenticed in a regional town or in London. Alan Macfarlane [in *The Family Life of Ralph Josselin, A Seventeenth-Century Clergyman: An Essay in Historical Anthropology*] has suggested that, "at the level of family life," this widespread and peculiarly English custom of farming out adolescent children was "a mechanism for separating the generations at a time when there might otherwise have been considerable difficulty." "The changes in patterns of authority as the children approached adulthood would . . . be diminished." He speculates further that, at the collective level, "the whole process was a form of age ritual, a way of demarcating off age-boundaries by movement through space.

The family was a source of social stability, but most families were short-lived and unstable. Youth was geographically mobile, but most youths were given no opportunity to enjoy their liberty. In schools and in households, the masters of scholars, servants, and apprentices were to be their surrogate fathers. Thomas stresses that, "though many children left home early and child labour was thought indispensable, there was total hostility to the early achievement of economic independence." The material basis of that hostility was alarm about the increasing pressure of population on very limited and unreliable resources. One of its most significant results was delayed marriage: "Combined with strict prohibition on alternative forms of sexual activity, late marriage was the most obvious way in which youth was prolonged. For marriage was the surest test of adult status and on it hinged crucial differences in wages, dress, and economic independence" (Stone, *Family, Sex and Marriage*). Most Elizabethan youths and maidens were in their mid or late twenties by the time they entered Hymen's bands. When Touchstone quips that "the forehead of a married man [is] more honourable than the bare brow of a bachelor" (3.3.53–55), he is giving a sarcastic twist to a fundamental mark of status. And when, late in his pseudo-mock-courtship of Ganymede, Orlando remarks ruefully that he "can live no longer by thinking" (5.2.50), he is venting the constrained libido of Elizabethan youth. One of the critical facts about the Elizabethan life cycle—one not noted in Jaques's speech—was that a large and varied group of codes, customs, and institutions regulated "a separation between physiological puberty and social puberty" (Thomas, "Age and Authority"). "Youth," then, was the Elizabethan age category separating the end of childhood from the beginning of adulthood. It was a social threshold whose transitional nature was manifested in shifts of residence, activity, sexual feeling, and patriarchal authority.

The dialectic between Elizabethan dramatic form and social process is especially conspicuous in the triadic romance pattern of exile and return that underlies *As You Like It*. Here the characters' experience is a fictional analogue of both the theatrical and the social experiences of its audience. "The circle of this forest" (5.4.34) is equivalent to Shakespeare's Wooden O. When they enter the special space-time of the theatre, the playgoers have voluntarily and temporarily withdrawn from "this working-day world" (1.3.12) and put on "a holiday humour" (4.1.65–66). When they have been wooed to an atonement by the comedy, the Epilogue conducts them back across the threshold between the world of the theatre and the theatre of the world. The dramatic form of the characters' experience corresponds, then, not only to the theatrical experience of the play's audience but also to the social process of youth in the world that playwright, players, and playgoers share. In a playworld of romance, Orlando and Rosalind experience separation from childhood, journeying, posing and disguising, altered and confused relationships to parental figures, sexual ambiguity, and tension. The fiction provides projections for the past or ongoing youthful experiences of most of the people in Shakespeare's Elizabethan audience. The forest sojourn conducts Orlando and Rosalind from an initial situation of oppression and frustration to the threshold of interdependent new identities. In one sense, then, the whole process of romantic pastoral comedy—the movement into and out of Arden—is what Macfarlane calls "a form of age ritual, a way of demarcating off age-boundaries by movement through space." The characters' fictive experience is congruent with the ambiguous and therefore dangerous period of the Elizabethan life cycle that it betwixt and between physical puberty and social puberty.

V

Not only relationships between offspring and their genitors, or between youths and their elders, but any relationship between subordinate and superior males might take on an oedipal character in a patriarchal society. Orlando is perceived as a troublemaker by Oliver and Frederick; his conflicts are with the men who hold power in his world, with its insecure and ineffectual villains. "The old Duke is banished by his younger brother and the new Duke" (1.1.99–100). Old Adam has served Orlando's family "from seventeen years, till now almost fourscore" (2.3.71), but under Oliver he must endure "unregarded age in corners thrown" (1.1.42). It is precisely the elders abused by Frederick and Oliver who ally themselves to Orlando's oppressed youth. Adam gives to Orlando the life savings that were to have been the "foster-nurse" (2.3.40) of his old age; he makes his "young master" (1.1.2) his heir. The idealized relationship of Orlando and his old servant compensates for the loss or corruption of Orlando's affective ties to men of his own kin and class. But Adam's paternity is only a phase in the reconstitution of Orlando's social identity. In the process of revealing his lineage to the old Duke, Orlando exchanges the father-surrogate who was his own father's servant for the father-surrogate who was his own father's lord.

> If that you were the good Sir Rowland's son,
> As you have whisper'd faithfully you were,
> And as mine eye doth his effigies witness
> Most truly limn'd and living in your face,
> Be truly welcome hither. I am the duke
> That lov'd your father.
>
> (2.7.194–99)

The living son replaces his dead father in the affections of their lord. The Duke, who has no natural son, assumes the role of Orlando's patron, his social father: "Give me your hand / And let me all your fortunes understand" (2.7.202–3). Orlando's previous paternal benefactor has been supplanted: Adam neither speaks nor is mentioned again.

The reunion of the de Boys brothers is blessed by "the old Duke"; the circumstance which makes that reunion possible is Oliver's expulsion by "the new Duke." In Lodge's *Rosalynde,* the two kings are not kin. Shakespeare's departure from his immediate source unifies and intensifies the conflicts in the family and the polity. The old Duke who adopts Orlando in the forest has been disinherited by his own younger brother in the court; Frederick has forcibly made himself his brother's heir. In the course of the play, fratricide is attempted, averted, and repudiated in each sibling relationship. Tensions in the nuclear family and in the body politic are miraculously assuaged within the forest. The Duke addresses his first words to his "comates and brothers in exile" (2.1.1). The courtly decorum of hierarchy and deference may be relaxed in the forest, but it has not been abrogated; the Duke's "brothers in exile" remain courtiers and servants attendant upon his grace. An atmosphere of charitable community has been created among those who have temporarily lost or abandoned their normal social context; the sources of conflict inherent in the social order are by no means genuinely dissolved in the forest, but rather are translated into a quiet and sweet style. In the forest, the old usurped Duke is a comate and brother to his loyal subjects and a benevolent father to Orlando. The comedy establishes *brotherhood* as an ideal of social as well as sibling male relationships; at the same time, it reaffirms a positive, nurturing image of *fatherhood.* And because family and society are a synecdoche, the comedy can also work to mediate the ideological contradiction between spiritual fraternity and political patriarchy, between social communion and social hierarchy.

Like Richard of Gloucester, Claudius, Edmund, and Antonio, Frederick is a discontented younger brother whom Shakespeare makes the malevolent agent of his plot. Frederick generates action in *As You Like It* by banishing successively his elder brother, his niece, and his subject. Like his fellow villains, Frederick is the effective agent of a dramatic resolution which he himself does not intend; the tyrant's perverted will subserves the comic dramatist's providential irony. Frederick enforces the fraternal bond between Orlando and Oliver by holding Oliver responsible for Orlando on peril of his inheritance, forcing Oliver out to apprehend his brother. By placing Oliver in a social limbo akin to that suffered by Orlando, Frederick unwittingly creates the circumstances that lead to the brothers' reunion:

> DUKE FREDERICK: Thy lands and all things that thou dost call
> thine,
> Worth seizure, do we seize into our hands,
> Till thou canst quit thee by thy brother's mouth
> Of what we think against thee.
> OLIVER: O that your Highness knew my heart in this!
> I never lov'd my brother in my life.
> DUKE FREDERICK: More villain thou.
>
> (3.1.9–15)

Oliver has abused the letter and the spirit of Sir Rowland's will: "It was . . . charged my brother on his blessing to breed me well" (1.1.3–4). Frederick is Oliver's nemesis.

In the exchange I have just quoted, Frederick's attitude toward Oliver is one of *moral* as well as political superiority. His judgment of Oliver's villainy is sufficiently ironic to give us pause. Is the usurper in Frederick projecting onto Oliver his guilt for his own unbrotherliness? Or is the younger brother in him identifying with Orlando's domestic situation? In seizing Oliver's lands and all things that he calls his until Oliver's (younger) brother can absolve him, Frederick parodies his own earlier usurpation of his own elder brother. Frederick's initial seizure takes place before the play begins; its circumstances are never disclosed. We do better to observe Frederick's dramatic function than to search for his unconscious motives. Frederick actualizes the destructive consequences of younger brothers' deprivation and discontent, in the family and in society at large. The first scenes demonstrate that such a threat exists within Orlando himself. The threat is neutralized as soon as Orlando enters the good old Duke's comforting forest home; there his needs are immediately and bountifully gratified:

> DUKE SENIOR: What would you have? Your gentleness shall
> force,
> More than your force move us to gentleness.
> ORLANDO: I almost die for food, and let me have it.
> DUKE SENIOR: Sit down and feed, and welcome to our table.
> ORLANDO: Speak you so gently? Pardon me, I pray you.
> I thought that all things had been savage here,
>
> . . . .
>
> Let gentleness my strong enforcement be;
> In the which hope, I blush, and hide my sword.
>
> (2.7.102–7, 118–19)

What is latent and potential within Orlando is displaced onto Frederick and realized in his violence and insecurity, his usurpation and tyranny. Frederick sustains the role of villain until he too comes to Arden:

> Duke Frederick hearing how that every day
> Men of great worth resorted to this forest,
> Address'd a mighty power, which were on foot
> In his own conduct, purposely to take
> His brother here, and put him to the sword.
> And to the skirts of this wild wood he came,
> Where, meeting with an old religious man,
> After some question with him, was converted
> Both from his enterprise and from the world,
> His crown bequeathing to his banish'd brother
> And all their lands restor'd to them again
> That were with him exil'd.
>
> (5.4.153–64)

Like Orlando, Frederick finds a loving father in the forest. And his conversion is the efficient cause of Orlando's elevation. In the denouement of Lodge's *Rosalynde,* the reunited brothers, Rosader and Saladyne, join the forces of the exiled King Gerismond; the army of the usurping King Torismond is defeated, and he is killed in the action. With striking formal and thematic economy, Shakespeare realizes his change of plot as a change *within* a character; he gets rid of Frederick not by killing him off but by morally transforming him. Frederick gives all his worldly goods to his natural brother and goes off to claim his spiritual inheritance from a heavenly father.

VI

The reunion of the de Boys brothers is narrated retrospectively by a reborn Oliver, in the alien style of an allegorical dream romance:

> Pacing through the forest,
> Chewing the food of sweet and bitter fancy,
> Lo what befell! He threw his eye aside,
> And mark that object did present itself.
> Under an old oak, whose boughs were moss'd with age
> And high top bald with dry antiquity,

> A wretched ragged man, o'ergrown with hair,
> Lay sleeping on his back.
>
> (4.3.100–107)

These images of infirm age and impotence, of regression to wildness and ruin through neglect, form a richly suggestive emblem. Expounded in the context of the present argument, the emblem represents the precarious condition into which fratricidal feeling provoked by primogeniture has brought these brothers and their house: "Such a fever hectic hath custome brought in and inured among fathers, and such fond desire they have to leave a great shewe of the *stock* of their house, though the *branches* be *withered,* that . . . my elder brother forsooth must be my master" (Thomas Wilson, *State of England, 1600,* [italics added]). Orlando, whose "having in beard is a younger brother's revenue" (3.2.367–68), confronts a hairy man asleep amidst icons of age and antiquity. The description suggests that, in confronting "his brother, his elder brother" (4.3.120), young Orlando is confronting a personification of his patriline and of the patriarchal order itself. The brothers find each other under an *arbor consanguinitatis,* at the de Boys "family tree."

Agnes Latham suggests that the snake and the lioness which menace Oliver are metaphors for his own animosities: as the snake "slides away, Oliver's envy melts, and his wrath goes with the lion." The text suggests that it is Orlando who undergoes such an allergorical purgation. When it sees Orlando, the snake slips under the bush where the lioness couches.

> OLIVER: This seen, Orlando did approach the man,
>   And found it was his brother, his elder brother.
> ROSALIND: But to Orlando. Did he leave him there,
>   Food to the suck'd and hungry lioness?
> OLIVER: Twice did he turn his back, and purpos'd so.
>   But kindness, nobler ever than revenge,
>   And nature, stronger than his just occasion,
>   Made him give battle to the lioness,
>   Who quickly fell before him; in which hurtling
>   From miserable slumber I awak'd.
>
> (4.3.119–20, 125–32)

In killing the lioness which threatens to kill Oliver, Orlando kills the impediment to atonement within himself. Oliver's narrative implies a casual relationship between Orlando's act of self-mastery and purgation and Oliver's own "awakening." When the brothers have been "kindly bath'd" (4.3.140) in mutual tears, Oliver's "conversion" (4.3.136) and his atonement with Orlando are consecrated by the Duke who loved their father. In the play's first words, Orlando remembered that Oliver had been charged, on his blessing, to breed him well. The Duke's bequest and injunction reformulate Sir Rowland's last will and testament:

> He led me to the gentle Duke,
> Who gave me fresh array and entertainment
> Committing me unto my brother's love.
>> (4.3.142–44)

What has taken place offstage is a conversion of the crucial event that precipitated the fraternal conflict, the event "remembered" in the very first words of the play.

At this point in the atonement, paternity and fraternity are reaffirmed as spiritual bonds rather than as bonds of blood and property. Brotherhood can now come to mean friendship freed from the material conflicts of kinship. Some remarks by Julian Pitt-Rivers illuminate the point:

> Kinship's nature . . . is not free of jural considerations. Rights and duties are distributed differentially to kinsmen because kinship is a system, not a network of dyadic ties like friendship. Status within it is ascribed by birth. . . . Rules of succession and inheritance are required to order that which cannot be left to the manifestations of brotherly love. . . . A revealing assertion echoes through the literature on ritual kinship: 'Blood-brothers are like brothers,' it is said, then comes, 'in fact they are closer than real brothers.' The implication is troubling, for it would appear that true fraternity is found only between those who are not real brothers. Amity does not everywhere enjoin the same open-ended generosity, least of all between kinsmen, who quarrel only too often, in contrast to ritual kinsmen, who are bound by sacred duty not to do so.
> ("The Kith and the Kin," in *The Character of Kinship*, ed. Jack Goody)

Before he goes to Arden, Orlando feels he has no alternative but to subject himself "to the malice / Of a diverted blood and bloody brother"

(2.3.36–37). Shakespeare's task is to bring the relationship of Orlando and Oliver under the auspices of Hymen:

> Then is there mirth in heaven,
> When earthly things made even
> Atone together.
>
> (5.4.107–9)

In Touchstone's terms (5.4.101–2), hostile siblings are brought to shake hands and swear their brotherhood by the virtue of comedy's If. The spiritual principle of "brotherly love" is reconciled to the jural principle of primogeniture; "real bothers" are made "blood brothers"—as the napkin borne by Oliver so graphically testifies.

Some commentators have seen the outlines of a Christian allegory of redemption in the play. They point to the presence of a character named Adam; the Duke's disquisition on "the penalty of Adam"; the iconography of the serpent, the tree, and the *vetus homo;* the heroic virtue of Orlando; the comic rite of atonement. Perhaps we do better to think of Shakespeare as creating resonances between the situations in his play and the religious archetypes at the foundations of his culture; as invoking what Rosalie Colie, writing of *King Lear,* calls "Biblical echo." What echoes deeply through the scenes I have discussed is the fourth chapter of Genesis, the story of Cain and Abel and what another of Shakespeare's fratricides calls "the primal eldest curse . . . / A brother's murther" (*Hamlet,* 3.3.37–38). Adam's two sons made offerings to the Lord: "and the Lord had respect unto Habel, and to his offering,"

> But unto Kain and to his offring he had no regarde: wherefore Kain was exceding wroth, & his countenance fel downe.
>
> Then the Lord said unto Kain, Why art thou wroth? and why is thy countenence cast downe?
>
> If thou do wel, shalt thou not be accepted? and if thou doest not well, sinne lieth at the dore: also unto thee his desire *shal be subject,* and thou shalt rule over him.
>
> Then Kain spake to Habel his brother. And when they were in the field, Kain rose up against Habel his brother, and slewe him.
>
> Then the Lord said unto Kain, Where is Habel thy brother? Who answered, I canot tel. Am I my brothers keper?

Againe he said, What hast thou done? the voyce of thy brothers blood cryeth unto me from the grounde.

Now therefore thou art cursed from the earth, which hath opened her mouth to receive thy brothers blood from thine hand.

(Gen. 4:4–11)

The Geneva Bible glosses the italicized phrase in the seventh verse as a reference to the foundations of primogeniture: "The dignitie of ye first borne is given to Kain over Habel."

The wrath of Cain echoes in Oliver's fratricidal musings at the end of the first scene: "I hope I shall see an end of him; for my soul—yet I know not why—hates nothing more than he. Yet he's gentle, never schooled and yet learned, full of noble device, of all sorts enchantingly beloved, and indeed so much in the heart of the world, and especially of my own people, that I am altogether misprised. But it shall not be so long" (1.1.162–69). Oliver feels humanly rather than divinely misprized; and it is his tyrannical secular lord to whom he declares that he is not his brother's keeper. Orlando sheds his own blood for his elder brother, which becomes the sign of Oliver's conversion rather than the mark of his fratricidal guilt. Oliver finds acceptance in the old Duke, who commits him to his brother's love. Shakespeare is creating a resonance between his romantic fiction and Biblical history, between the dramatic process of assuaging family conflict in the atonements of comedy and the exegetical process of redeeming the primal fratricide of Genesis in the spiritual fraternity of the Gospel:

For brethren, ye have bene called unto libertie: onely use not *your* libertie as an occasion unto the flesh, but by love serve one another.

For all the Law is fulfilled in one worde, which is this, Thou shalt love thy neighbour as thy self.

If ye byte & devoure one another, take hede lest ye be consumed one of another.

Then I say, walke in the Spirit, and ye shal not fulfil the lustes of the flesh.

(Galatians 5:13–16)

The rivalry or conflict between elder and younger brothers is a prominent motif in the fictions of cultures throughout the world. Its typical plot has been described as "the disadvantaged younger sibling or orphan child besting an unjust elder and gaining great fortune through the timely intercession of a benevolent supernatural being." Cultural fictions of the triumphs of younger siblings offer psychological compensation for the social fact of the deprivation of younger siblings. Such fictions are symbolic mediations of discrepancies between the social categories of status and the claims of individual merit, in which the defeat and supplanting of the elder sibling by the younger reconciles ability with status: "The younger outwits, displaces, and becomes the elder; the senior position comes to be associated with superior ability."

The folk-tale scenario of sibling rivalry is clear in the fourteenth-century tale of *Gamelyn,* to which Lodge's Rosader plot and Shakespeare's Orlando plot are indebted. The disinherited Gamelyn and his outlaw cohorts sentence Gamelyn's eldest brother to death by hanging. Their topsy-turvy actions are sanctioned and absorbed by the social order: the King pardons Gamelyn, restores his inheritance, and makes him Chief Justice. In *As You Like It,* Shakespeare's characters emphasize the discrepancy between "the gifts of the world" and "the lineaments of Nature" (1.2.40–41), between social place and personal merit. The comedy's task is to "mock the good hussif Fortune from her wheel, that her gifts may henceforth be bestowed equally" (1.2.30–32). Shakespeare transcends *Gamelyn* and its folktale paradigm in a wholehearted concern not merely to eliminate social contradictions, but also to redeem and reconcile human beings. Oliver is not defeated, eliminated, supplanted; he is converted, reintegrated, confirmed. In the subplot of *King Lear,* the unbrotherly struggle for mastery and possession is resolved by fratricide; the comic resolution of *As You Like It* depends instead upon an expansion of opportunities for mastery and possession.

VII

In Lodge's *Rosalynde,* the crude heroic theme of *Gamelyn* is already fused with the elegant love theme of Renaissance pastorals. In constructing a romantic comedy of familial and sexual tension resolved in brotherhood and marriage, Shakespeare gives new complexity and cohesiveness to his narrative source. The struggle of elder and younger brothers is not simply duplicated; it is inverted. In the younger generation, the elder brother abuses the younger; in the older generation, the younger abuses the elder. The range of experience and affect is thereby enlarged, and the protest against primogeniture is firmly balanced by its reaffirmation. Myth, Scripture, and Shakespearean drama record "the bond crack'd betwixt son and father" (*King Lear* 1.2.113–14). Hostilities between elder and younger brothers and between fathers and sons are homologous: "Yea, and the brother shal deliver the brother to death, and the father the sonne, and the children shal rise against their parents, and shal cause them to dye" (Mark 13.14). Because in *As You Like It* the doubling and inversion of fraternal conflict links generations, the relationship of brother and brother can be linked to the relationship of father and son. In the process of atonement, the two families and two generations of men are doubly and symmetrically bound: the younger brother weds the daughter of the elder brother, and the elder brother weds the daughter of the younger brother. They create the figure of *chiasmus*. Whatever vicarious benefit *As You Like It* brings to younger brothers and to youths, it is not achieved by perverting or destroying the bonds between siblings and between generations, but by transforming and renewing them— *through marriage*.

In Arden, Orlando divides his time between courting Rosalind (who is played by Ganymede, who is played by Rosalind) and courting the old Duke who is Rosalind's father. Celia teases Rosalind about the sincerity of Orlando's passion, the truth of his feigning, by reminding her of his divided loyalties: "He attends here in the forest on the Duke your father" (3.4.29–30). Rosalind, who clearly resents that she must share Orlando's attentions with her father, responds: "I met the Duke yesterday and had much question with him. He asked me of what parentage I was: I told him of as good as he, so he laughed and let me go. But what talk we of fathers, when there is such a man as Orlando?" (3.4.31–35). Celia has already transferred her loyalties from her father to Rosalind; Rosalind is transferring hers from her father and from Celia to Orlando. But she withholds her identity from her lover in order to test and to taunt him. In the forest, while Orlando guilelessly improves his place in the patriarchal order, Rosalind wittily asserts her independence of it. Rosalind avoids her father's recognition and establishes her own household within the forest; Orlando desires the Duke's recognition and gladly serves him in his forest-court.

It is only after he has secured a place within the old Duke's benign all male community that Orlando begins to play the lover and the poet: "Run, run Orlando, carve on every tree / The fair, the chaste, and unexpressive she" (3.2.9–10):

> But upon the fairest boughs,
> Or at every sentence end,
> Will I Rosalinda write,
> Teaching all that read to know
> The quintessence of every sprite
> Heaven would in little show.
> Therefore Heaven Nature charg'd
> That one body should be fill'd
> With all graces wide-enlarg'd.
> Nature presently distill'd
> Helen's cheek, but not her heart,
> Cleopatra's majesty,
> Atalanta's better part,
> Sad Lucretia's modesty.
> Thus Rosalind of many parts
> By heavenly synod was devis'd,
> Of many faces, eyes, and hearts,
> To have the touches dearest priz'd.
> Heaven would that she these gifts should have,
> And I to live and die her slave.
>
> (3.2.132–51)

The Petrarchan lover "writes" his mistress or "carves" her in the image of his own desire, incorporating virtuous feminine stereotypes and scrupulously excluding what is sexually threatening. The lover masters his mistress by inscribing her within his own discourse; he worships a deity of his own making and under his control. When Rosalind-Ganymede confronts this "fancy-monger" (3.2.354–55) who "haunts the forest . . . deifying the name of Rosalind" (3.2.350, 353–54), she puts a question to him: "But are you so much in love as your rhymes speak?" (3.2.386). Rosalind and Touchstone interrogate and undermine self-deceiving amorous rhetoric with bawdy wordplay and relentless insistence upon the power and inconstancy of physical desire. All the love-talk in the play revolves around the issue of mastery in the shifting social relationship between the sexes: in courtship, maidens suspect the faithfulness of their suitors; in wedlock, husbands suspect the faithfulness of their wives. The poems of feigning lovers and the horns of cuckolded husbands are the complementary preoccupations of Arden's country copulatives.

Consider the crucially-placed brief scene (4.2) which is barely more than a song inserted between the betrothal scene of Orlando and Rosalind-Ganymede and the scene in which Oliver comes to Rosalind bearing the bloody napkin. In 4.1, Rosalind mocks her tardy lover with talk of an emblematic snail: "He brings his destiny with him. . . . Horns—which such as you fain to be beholding to your wives for" (4.1.54–55, 57–58). Touchstone has already resigned himself to the snail's destiny with his own misogynistic logic: "As horns are odious, they are necessary. It is said, many a man knows no end of his goods. Right. Many a man has good horns and knows no end of them. Well, that is the dowry of his wife, 'tis none of his own getting" (3.3.45–49). Now, in 4.2, Jaques transforms Rosalind's jibes into ironic male self-mockery: "He that killed the deer" is to have the horns set on his head "for a branch of victory" (4.2.1, 5). Jaques calls for a song— " 'Tis no matter how it be in tune, so it makes noise enough" (4.2.8–9). The rowdy horn song is a kind of *charivari* or "rough music," traditionally the form of ridicule to which cuckolds and others who offended the community's moral standards were subjected. This *charivari,* however, is also a song of consolation and good fellowship, for not only the present "victor" but all his companions "shall bear this burden" (4.2.12–13).

> Take thou no scorn to wear the horn,
> It was a crest ere thou wast born.
> Thy father's father wore it,
> And thy father bore it.
> The horn, the horn, the lusty horn,
> Is not a thing to laugh to scorn.
>
> (4.2.14–19)

The play's concern with patriarchal lineage and the hallmarks of gentility is here transformed into an heraldic celebration of the horn— instrument of male potency and male degradation—which marks all men as kinsmen. Thus, although cuckoldry implies the uncertainty of paternity, the song celebrates the paradox that it is precisely the common destiny they share with the snail that binds men together—father to son, brother to brother. Through the metaphor of hunting (with its wordplays on "deer" and "horns") and the medium of song, the threat that the power of insubordinate women poses to the authority of men is transformed into an occasion for affirming and celebrating patriarchy and fraternity.

After the mock-marriage (4.1) in which they have indeed plighted their troth, Rosalind-Ganymede exuberantly teases Orlando about the shrewishness and promiscuity he can expect from his wife. Naively romantic Orlando abruptly leaves his threatening Rosalind in order "to attend the Duke at dinner" (4.1.170). On his way from his cruel mistress to his kind patron, Orlando encounters his own brother. It is hardly insignificant that Shakespeare changes the details of the fraternal recognition scene to include an aspect of sexual differentiation wholly absent from Lodge's romance. He adds the snake which wreathes itself around Oliver's neck; and he makes it into an insidious female, "who with her head, nimble in threats, approach'd / The opening of his mouth" (4.3.109–10). Furthermore, he changes Lodge's lion into a lioness whose nurturing and aggressive aspects are strongly and ambivalently stressed: "a lioness, with udders all drawn dry" (4.3.114); "the suck'd and hungry lioness" (4.3.126). Orlando has retreated in the face of Rosalind's verbal aggressiveness. He has wandered through the forest, "chewing the food of sweet and bitter fancy" (4.3.101), to seek the paternal figure who has nurtured him. Instead, he has found Oliver in a dangerously passive condition, threatened by a double source of oral aggression.

Oliver's fantastic narrative suggests a transformation of the sexual conflict initiated by Rosalind when she teases Orlando in 4.1. Rosalind and the lioness are coyly linked in the exchange between the lovers at their next meeting:

ROSALIND: O my dear Orlando, how it grieves me to see
    thee wear thy heart in a scarf!
ORLANDO: It is my arm.
ROSALIND: I thought thy heart had been wounded with the
    claws of a lion.
ORLANDO: Wounded it is, but with the eyes of a lady.
                                    (5.2.19–23)

The chain which Rosalind bestows upon Orlando at their first meeting ("Wear this for me" [1.2.236]) is the mark by which Celia identifies him in the forest ("And a chain, that you once wore, about his neck" [3.2.178]). The "green and gilded snake" (4.3.108) encircling Oliver's neck is a demonic parody of the emblematic stage property worn by his brother throughout the play. The gynephobic response to Rosalind is split into the erotic serpent and the maternal lioness, while Orlando is split into his victimized brother and his heroic self. Orlando's mastery of the lioness ("Who quickly fell before him" [4.3.131]) is, then, a symbolic mastery of Rosalind's challenge to Orlando. But it is also a triumph of fraternal "kindness" (4.3.128) over the fratricidal impulse. Relationships between elder and younger brothers and between fathers and sons are purified by what the text suggests is a kind of matricide, a triumph of men over female powers. Thus the killing of the lioness may also symbolize a repudiation of the consanguinity of Orlando and Oliver. If this powerful female—the carnal source of siblings—is destroyed, both fraternity and paternity can be reconceived as male relationships unmediated by woman, relationships of the spirit rather than of the flesh. Orlando's heroic act, distanced and framed in an allegorical narrative, condenses aspects of both the romantic plot and the sibling plot. And these plots are themselves the complementary aspects of a single social and dramatic process.

Before Orlando is formally married to Rosalind at the end of the play, he has reaffirmed his fraternal and filial bonds in communion with other men. Orlando's rescue of Oliver from the she-snake and the lioness frees the brothers' capacity to give and to receive love. Now Oliver can "fall in love" with Celia; and now Orlando "can live no longer by thinking" (5.2.50) about Rosalind. Oliver asks his younger brother's consent to marry, and resigns to him his birthright: "My father's house and all the revenue that was old Sir Rowland's will I estate upon you, and here live and die a shepherd" (5.2.10–12). Orlando agrees with understandable alacrity: "You have my consent. Let your wedding be tomorrow" (5.2.13–14). Marriage, the social institution at the heart of comedy, serves to ease or eliminate fraternal strife. And fraternity, in turn, serves as a defense against the threat men feel from women.

Rosalind-as-Ganymede and Ganymede-as-Rosalind—the woman out of place—exerts an informal organizing and controlling power over affairs in the forest. But this power lapses when she relinquishes her male disguise and formally acknowledges her normal status as daughter and wife: "I'll have no father, if you be not he. / I'll have no husband, if you be not he" (5.4.121–22). In a ritual gesture of surrender, she assumes the passive role of mediatrix between the Duke and Orlando:

> [*To the Duke.*] To you I give myself, for I am yours.
> [*To Orlando.*] To you I give myself, for I am yours.
> (5.4.115–16)

The Duke's paternal bond to Orlando is not established through the natural fertility of a mother but through the supernatural virginity of a daughter: "Good Duke receive thy daughter, / Hymen from heaven brought her" (5.4.110–11). The play is quite persistent in creating strategies for subordinating the flesh to the spirit, and female powers to male controls. Hymen's marriage rite gives social sanction to the lovers' mutual desire. But the atonement of man and woman also implies the social subordination of wife to husband. Rosalind's exhilarating mastery of herself and others has been a compensatory "holiday humor," a temporary, inversionary rite of misrule, whose context is a transfer of authority, property, and title from the Duke to his prospective male heir. From the perspective of the present argument, the romantic love plot serves more than its own ends: it is also the means by which other actions are transformed and resolved. In his unions with the Duke and with Rosalind, Orlando's social elevation is confirmed. Such a perspective does not deny the comedy its festive magnanimity; it merely reaffirms that Shakespearean drama registers the form and pressure of Elizabethan experience. If *As You Like It* is a vehicle for Rosalind's exuberance, it is also a structure for her containment.

Jaques de Boys, "the second son of old Sir Rowland" (5.4.151), enters suddenly at the end of the play. This Shakespearean whimsy fits logically into the play's comic process. As the narrator of Frederick's strange eventful history, Jaques brings the miraculous news that resolves the conflict between his own brothers as well as the conflict between the brother-dukes. As Rosalind mediates the affinity of father and son, so Jaques—a brother, rather than a mother—mediates the kinship of eldest and youngest brothers; he is, in effect, the incarnate middle term between Oliver and Orlando. The Duke welcomes him:

> Thou offer'st fairly to thy brothers' wedding;
> To one his lands withheld, and to the other
> A land itself at large, a potent dukedom.
>
> (5.4.166–68)

Jaques's gift celebrates the wedding of his brothers to their wives and to each other. Solutions to the play's initial conflicts are worked out between brother and brother, father and son—among men. Primogeniture is reaffirmed in public and private domains: the Duke, newly restored to his own authority and possessions, now restores the de Boys patrimony to Oliver. The aspirations and deserts of the youngest brother are rewarded when the Duke acknowledges Orlando as his own heir, the successor to property, power, and title that far exceed Oliver's birthright. The eldest brother regains the authority due him by primogeniture at the same time that the youngest brother is freed from subordination to his sibling and validated in his claim to the perquisites of gentility.

With his patrimony restored and his marriage effected, Oliver legitimately assumes the place of a patriarch and emerges into full social adulthood; he is now worthy to be the son and heir of Sir Rowland de Boys. Orlando, on the other hand, has proved himself worthy to become son and heir to the Duke. Thomas Wilson, another Elizabethan younger brother, made the bitter misfortune of primogeniture the spur to personal achievement: "This I must confess doth us good someways, for it makes us industrious to apply ourselves to letters or to armes, whereby many time we become my master elder brothers' masters, or at least their betters in honour and reputacion." Unlike Thomas Wilson, Shakespeare's Orlando is spectacularly successful, and his success is won more by spontaneous virtue than by industry. But like Wilson's, Orlando's accomplishments are those of a gentleman and a courtier. Unlike most Elizabethan younger sons, Orlando is not forced to descend to commerce or to labor to make his way in the world. He succeeds by applying himself to the otiose courtship of his mistress and his prince. Although the perfection of his social identity is deferred during the Duke's lifetime, Orlando's new filial subordination is eminently beneficent. It grants him by affinity what he has been denied by kinship: the social advancement and sexual fulfillment of which youths and younger sons were so frequently deprived. The de Boys brothers atone together when the eldest replaces a father and the youngest recovers a father.

VIII

Social and dramatic decorum require that, "to work a comedy kindly, grave old men should instruct, young men should show the imperfections of youth" London's city fathers, however, were forever accusing the theatres and the plays of corrupting rather than instructing youth: "We verely think plays and theatres to be the cheif cause . . . of . . . disorder & lewd demeanours which appear of late in young people of all degrees." Shakespeare's play neither preaches to youths nor incites them to riot. In the world of its Elizabethan audience, the form of Orlando's experience may indeed have functioned as a collective compensation, a projection for the wish-fulfillment fantasies of younger brothers, youths, and all who felt themselves deprived by their fathers or their fortunes. But Orlando's mastery of adversity could also provide support and encouragement to the ambitious individuals who identified with his plight. The play may have fostered strength and perseverance as much as it facilitated pacification and escape. For the large number of youths in Shakespeare's audience—firstborn and younger siblings, gentle and base—the performance may have been analogous to a rite of passage, helping to ease their dangerous and prolonged journey from subordination to identity, their difficult transition from the child's part to the adult's.

My subject has been the complex interrelationship of brothers, fathers, and sons in *As You Like It*. But I have suggested that the play's concern with relationships among men is only artificially separable from its concern with relationships between men and women. The androgynous Rosalind—boy actor and princess—addresses Shakespeare's heterosexual audience in an epilogue: "My way is to conjure you, and I'll begin with the women. I charge you, O women, for the love you bear to men, to like as much of this play as please you. And I charge you, O men, for the love you bear to women—as I perceive by your simpering none of you hates them—that between you and the women the play may please" (5.4.208–14). Through the subtle and flexible strategies of drama—in puns, jokes, games, disguises, songs, poems, fantasies—*As You Like It* expresses, contains, and discharges a measure of the strife between the men and the women. Shakespeare's comedy manipulates the differential social relationships between the sexes, between brothers, between father and son, master and servant, lord and subject. It is by the conjurer's art that Shakespeare manages to reconcile the social imperatives of hierarchy and difference with the festive urges toward leveling and atonement. The intense and ambivalent personal bonds upon which the play is focused—bonds between brothers and between lovers—affect each other reciprocally and become the means of each other's resolution. And as the actions within the play are dialectically related to each other, so the world of Shakespeare's characters is dialectically related to the world of his audience. *As You Like It* is both a theatrical *reflection* of social conflict and a theatrical *source* of social conciliation.

Sexual Politics and Social Structure in *As You Like It*

Peter Erickson

The dramatic and emotional effect of Shakespearean comedy can be defined as a process of making manifest "a tough reasonableness beneath the slight lyric grace." This comic toughness derives in part from Shakespeare's ability to mix genres, an ability that helps to account for his artistic power. In exploring Shakespeare's use of genre, we must be concerned as much with overlapping as with differentiation. The father-son motif, for example, provides a specific point of contact between *As You Like It* and *Henry V*. The analogous relationships between Duke Senior and Orlando in the first play and Henry IV and Hal in the second help to cut across an oversimplified generic distinction that says history plays deal with political power (implicitly understood as male power) whereas comedies treat love. Rosalind's androgynous allure can appear so attractive, her linguistic virtuosity so engaging, that all our attention becomes focused on her, as if nothing else happened or mattered. Her talking circles around Orlando seems sufficient proof of her complete triumph. Yet this line of response is deficient because it ignores important parts of the play; that is, political power is a significant element in *As You Like It*.

The transmission of paternal heritage, announced at the outset in Orlando's lament, begins to receive fulfillment when Orlando fashions an alliance with Duke Senior in the forest when no women are present.

From *Patriarchal Structures in Shakespeare's Drama*. © 1982 by the Massachusetts Review, Inc., © 1985 by the Regents of the University of California. University of California Press, 1985.

After his initial complaint about being deprived of a "good education" (1.1.67–68), Orlando is educated twice: once by Rosalind's father and then by Rosalind. The exiles in the forest can indulge in the pleasures of melancholy because the play can amply satisfy the need for true versions of debased human relationship: "Most friendship is feigning, most loving mere folly" (2.7.181). We relish the platitude of this general rule in order to appreciate the magic of the exceptions. But the question still remains: how are the twin themes of friendship and loving coordinated with each other? And an exclusive focus on Rosalind prevents our asking it. Male friendship, exemplified by the reconciliation of Duke Senior and Orlando, provides a framework that diminishes and contains Rosalind's apparent power. My point is not that *As You Like It* is a history play in disguise or that there are no differences between genres. The pastoral feast in the forest of Arden is far less stressful than the feast of Crispian that Henry V imagines as an antidote to the disturbing memory of his inheritance through "the fault / My father made in compassing the crown" (*H5*, 4.1.293–94). Unlike Henry V, Orlando is never made to confront a paternal fault. However, an exaggerated contrast between history and comedy is misleading. Concentration on Rosalind to the neglect of other issues distorts the overall design of *As You Like It,* one that is governed by male ends.

I

The endings of *Love's Labor's Lost* and *As You Like It* present a striking contrast. In the earlier play, Berowne comments explicitly on the absence of marriage and closure, for which, in his frustration, he holds the women responsible: "Our wooing doth not end like an old play: / Jack hath not Gill. These ladies' courtesy / Might well have made our sport a comedy" (5.2.874–76). *Love's Labor's Lost* culminates in the failure of courtship, but *As You Like It* reaches a fully and flamboyantly festive conclusion with the onstage revelation of the symbol of marital union, Hymen, who presides over a quadruple wedding. The prevailing mood of sourness at the end of *Love's Labor's Lost* is held in check in the later play by confining the potential for bitterness and disruption to Jaques, the nonparticipant. But even Jaques generously acknowledges the validity of love when he gives his blessing to Orlando, whom he had formerly mocked as "Signior Love" (3.2.292): "You to a love, that your true faith doth merit" (5.4.188).

In the final scene of *Love's Labor's Lost,* festivity is short-circuited.

The concluding masques and songs are no more helpful in facilitating the happy ending than the men's poetry had been earlier. The masques of the Muscovites and of the Nine Worthies are farcical artistic performances that precipitate discord. "More Ates, more Ates! stir them on, stir them on!" (5.2.688–89), cries Berowne in an enthusiastic effort to provoke violence between Costard and Armado. Nor do the companion songs of the cuckoo and the owl dispel the awkward atmosphere. The songs act as a conspicuously inadequate substitute for the consummation that has failed to occur among the main characters. The alternative presented by the songs twits the anxiety it ostensibly seeks to mitigate by invoking the larger perspective of the natural cycle:

> The cuckoo then on every tree
> Mocks married men; for thus sings he,
> > "Cuckoo;
> Cuckoo, cuckoo"—O word of fear,
> Unpleasing to a married ear!
> > (5.2.898–902)

This apparently blithe epilogue mirrors the men's situation in the play proper by restating women's power to make or break men. It recapitulates but does not relieve the humiliation of men as helpless victims of female caprice.

By contrast, *As You Like It* creates a context in which the efficaciousness of art is affirmed rather than denied. The masque of Hymen anticipates the sanctified unity of a late romance by appealing to the trope of "wonder":

> Whiles a wedlock-hymn we sing,
> Feed yourselves with questioning;
> That reason wonder may diminish
> How thus we met, and these things finish.
> > (5.4.137–40)

The equation of wedding with formal closure is indicated by Hymen's ostentatious use of words like "finish" and "conclusion": "Peace ho! I bar confusion, / 'Tis I must make conclusion" (125–26). This gratifying happy ending is convincing, however, because Hymen's role is not just a matter of external *deus ex machina*. In presenting Rosalind undisguised, the god of marriage claims that "Hymen from heaven brought her" (112), but we are entitled to feel that the reverse is true: Rosalind has brought Hymen. The character of Rosalind, the real coordinator of the final scene, stands behind the metaphor of magic she invokes for the play's resolution: "Believe then, if you please, that I can do strange things. I have, since I was three year old, convers'd with a magician, most profound in his art, and yet not damnable" (5.2.58–61). Rosalind has explored the limits of the magic that her male costume has afforded her in the forest of Arden. Like Prospero, she now gives up this magic, but she has earned her final throwaway use of it.

This comparative sketch of the endings of *Love's Labor's Lost* and *As You Like It* raises questions. How do we account for the difference between the two endings? How is the resolution of *As You Like It* achieved? A partial answer lies in Shakespeare's use of pastoral. In *Love's Labor's Lost,* pastoral applies only to the setting and general atmosphere but does not extend to the dramatic structure. The play sets up a contrast between two worlds: the court in which the men take refuge versus the field which the women insist on making their residence. However, the relationship between the two worlds is one of simple opposition. The static quality of this relationship leaves too little room for interplay between the worlds and leads directly to the stalemate of the conclusion. *As You Like It* dramatically expands the contrast and the possibilities for interaction between the two worlds of court and forest. The sharply differentiated landscapes unfold in sequence, making it possible for men to enter the green world and creating the dynamic three-part process identified by Barber and Northrop Frye. This full realization of pastoral form in *As You Like It* gives Shakespeare an artistic leverage on his material that helps to make possible the final resolution.

While useful, this kind of structural comparison can take us only so far. Formal description is insufficient as a total explanation of the differences between *Love's Labor's Lost* and *As You Like It* because the respective uneasiness and confidence of their endings is a matter of the relations between men and women as well as of aesthetic form. Hence it becomes imperative to look at the plays from the perspective of sexual politics. From this perspective, Shakespeare's development from *Love's Labor's Lost* to *As You Like It* does not emerge as the unqualified advancement it might otherwise appear to be. The ending of *As You Like It* works smoothly because male control is affirmed and women are rendered nonthreatening whereas in *Love's Labor's Lost* women do not surrender their independence and the status of patriarchy remains in doubt. Harmony and disharmony have as much to do with the specific content of male-female relations as with aesthetic form.

In both *Love's Labor's Lost* and *As You Like It,* love brings out a disparity between male and female intelligence and power. Orlando, like the four lords, is transformed in a way that makes him look humorously but embarrassingly naïve and helpless. Falling in love is experienced as incapacitation:

> My better parts
> Are all thrown down, and that which here stands up
> Is but a quintain, a mere liveless block.
>
> . . . .
>
> O poor Orlando! thou art overthrown
> Or Charles, or something weaker, masters thee.
>
> (1.2.249–51, 259–60)

His sense of being mastered helps to create a one-sided relationship in which the woman has control. Again like the four lords, Orlando equates being in love with the reflex gesture of producing huge quantities of poetry, and he follows a poetic convention that further increases the woman's power:

> Thus Rosalind of many parts
>   By heavenly synod was devis'd
> Of many faces, eyes, and hearts,
>   To have the touches dearest priz'd.
> Heaven would that she these gifts should have,
> And I to live and die her slave.
>
> (3.2.149–54)

The mechanical and impersonal nature of this elevation of the woman to divine status is demonstrated by the way Orlando's poem invents her through an amalgamation of fantasized "parts." Worship of the woman that is supposed to pay homage creates an inhuman pastiche that demeans her and inhibits genuine contact. Such obeisance also belittles the man since Orlando's poem defines a sharply hierarchical relationship in which his idealization of Rosalind as the perfect goddess leaves him with the role—exaggerated in the opposite direction—of "slave." The servility implied by poetic worship is taken a step further in the case of Silvius, whose "holy" and "perfect" love make him content "To glean the broken ears after the man / That the main harvest reaps" (3.5.99, 102–3). Rosalind's observation that Orlando's verse is "lame" (3.2.168) refers not only to the poem's execution but also to the psychological stance Orlando adopts toward her.

Rosalind is thus placed in a position parallel to that of the ladies in *Love's Labor's Lost*. Like them, she is strong and manipulative as she uses her superior wit along with the advantages given to her by circumstance to disabuse Orlando of his stock notions of male and female roles in love. There is, however, a vast difference in the outcome of this process in the two plays because Rosalind proves to be more flexible and accommodating than the women of *Love's Labor's Lost*. Her response to Phebe and Silvius is an attack on sonnet convention that implicitly involves a self-education for Rosalind. In upbraiding the two for their enactment of the stereotype of female scorn and male abasement, she is as critical of Silvius (3.5.49–56) as of Phebe. Rosalind's effort to put Phebe in her place is accompanied by her attempt to bring Silvius up to his place. This double lesson has an application to her own behavior since Rosalind's decision to "speak to him like a saucy lackey, and under that habit to play the knave with him" (3.2.295–97) carries the danger that she will allow herself to be as "proud and pitiless" (3.5.40) as she accuses Phebe of being, while Orlando languishes in Silvius-like submissiveness. Observing this dynamic at work in another relation alerts her to the potential Phebe in herself. Rosalind thus proves a more "busy actor in their play" (3.4.59) than she had anticipated; her fervent effort to convince Phebe to adopt more tractable behavior becomes an argument that she must accept her own advice. Rosalind's capacity to give up this pride is what allows *As You Like It* to extricate itself from the poetic postures of male subservience and female omnipotence in which *Love's Labor's Lost* remains fixed to the bitter end.

If Rosalind's flexibility is the key reason that *As You Like It* ends "like an old play" with "Jack having his Gill," we must go on to ask: what is the nature of this flexibility? and is the absence of it in *Love's Labor's Lost* entirely in *As You Like It*'s favor? The standard approach stresses that Rosalind has a larger emotional range than the ladies of *Love's Labor's Lost*. She is more impressive because more complex and more humane. The encounter between Rosalind and Jaques at the beginning of act 4, scene 1, makes clear her rejection of his detachment: "I fear you have sold your own lands to see other men's; then to have seen much, and to have nothing, is to have rich eyes and poor hands" (22–25). Her direct experience and involvement distinguish her from the women of *Love's Labor's Lost,* who in the end "have nothing." But a second approach sees Rosalind as a woman who submits to a man who is her inferior. The power symbolized by her male costume is only temporary, and the harmonious conclusion is based on her willingness to relinquish this power. Thus Rosalind's passionate involvement has a significant negative side since involvement means co-option and assimilation by a society ruled by men. She escapes the female stereotype of the all-powerful woman created by lyrical inflation only at the price of succumbing to another stereotype: the compliant, essentially powerless woman fostered by practical patriarchal politics.

Before entering the forest of Arden, Rosalind's companion Celia/ Aliena redefines this pastoral space to mean opportunity rather than punishment: "Now go we in content / To liberty, and not to banishment" (1.3.137–38). This "liberty" implies overcoming the restrictions of the female role. The idea of the male disguise originates as a strategy for avoiding the normal vulnerability to male force: "Alas, what danger will it be to us, / Maids as we are, to travel forth so far! / Beauty provoketh thieves sooner than gold" (108–10). Rosalind's male costume, as it evolves, expands her identity so that she can play both male and female roles. Yet the costume is problematic. Though it gives her freedom of action and empowers her to take the initiative with Orlando, it simultaneously serves as a protective device, which temptingly offers excessive security, even invulnerability. In order to love, Rosalind must reveal herself directly to Orlando, thereby making herself vulnerable. She must give up the disguise and appear—as she ultimately promises Orlando—"human as she is" (5.2.67). But in giving up the disguise, she also gives up the strength it symbolizes. As the disguise begins to break down before its official removal, Rosalind's transparent femininity takes the form of fainting—a sign of weakness that gives her away: "You a man? / You lack a man's heart" (4.3.163–64). This loss of control signals that Rosalind can no longer deny her inner feminine self. The capacity for love that we find so admirable in Rosalind is compromised by the necessity that she resume a traditional female role in order to engage in love.

This traditional image has been present all along. Rosalind willingly confides to Celia that she remains a woman despite the male costume: "in my heart / Lie there what hidden woman's fear there will— / We'll have a swashing and a martial outside" (1.3.118–20); "Good my complexion, dost thou think, though I am caparison'd like a man, I have a doublet and hose in my disposition?" (3.2.194–96); and "Do you not know I am a woman?" (249). By virtue of the costume,

Rosalind does have access to both male and female attributes, but the impression she conveys of androgynous wholeness is misleading. Neither Rosalind nor the play questions the conventional categories of masculine and feminine. She does not reconcile gender definitions in the sense of integrating or synthesizing them. Her own insistence on the metaphor of exterior (male) and interior (female) keeps the categories distinct and separable. The liberation that Rosalind experiences in the forest has built into it the conservative countermovement by which, as the play returns to the normal world, she will be reduced to the traditional woman who is subservient to men.

Rosalind is shown working out in advance the terms of her return. Still protected by her disguise yet allowing herself to come closer to the decisive moment, she instructs Orlando to "woo me" (4.1.68) and subsequently tells him what to say in a wedding rehearsal while she practises yielding. Though she teases Orlando with the wife's power to make him a cuckold and then to conceal her duplicity with her "wayward wit" (160–76), this is good fun, and it is only that. It is clear to the audience, if not yet to Orlando, that Rosalind's flaunting of her role as disloyal wife is a put-on rather than a genuine threat. She may playfully delay the final moment when she becomes a wife, but we are reassured that, once married, she will in fact be faithful. Her humor has the effect of exorcising and renouncing her potential weapon. The uncertainty concerns not her loyalty but Orlando's, as her sudden change of tone when he announces his departure indicates: "Alas, dear love, I cannot lack thee two hours!" (178). Her exuberance and control collapse in fears of his betrayal: "Ay, go your ways, go your ways; I knew what you would prove" (182–83). Her previous wit notwithstanding, for Rosalind the scene is less a demonstration of power than an exercise in vulnerability. She is once again consigned to anxious waiting for her tardy man: "But why did he swear he would come this morning, and comes not?" (3.4.18–19).

Rosalind's own behavior neutralizes her jokes about cuckoldry, but this point is sharply reinforced by the brief account of the male hunt that immediately follows act 4, scene 1. The expected negative meaning of horns as the sign of a cuckold is transformed into a positive image of phallic potency that unites men. Changing the style of his literary response to deer killing, Jaques replaces his earlier lament (2.1.26–66) with a celebration of male hunt and conquest: "Let's present him to the Duke like a Roman conqueror, and it would do well to set the deer's horns upon his head, for a branch of victory" (4.2.3–5).

The rousing song occasioned by this moment suggests the power of an all-male activity to provide a self-sufficient male heritage, thus to defend against male insecurity about humiliation by women.

The final scene, orchestrated by Rosalind, demonstrates her power in a paradoxical way. She is the architect of a resolution that phases out the control she has wielded and prepares the way for the patriarchal status quo. She accedes to the process by which, in the transition from courtship to marriage, power passes from the female to the male: the man is no longer the suitor who serves, obeys, and begs but is now the husband who commands. Rosalind's submission is explicit but not ironic, though her tone may be high-spirited. To each of the two men in her life she declares: "To you I give myself, for I am yours" (5.4.116–17). Her casting herself in the role of male possession is all the more charming because she does not have to be forced to adopt it: her self-taming is voluntary. We may wish to give Rosalind credit for her cleverness in forestalling male rivalry between her father and her fiancé. Unlike Cordelia, she is smart enough to see that in order to be gratified, each man needs to feel that he is the recipient of all her love, not half of it. Yet Rosalind is not really in charge here because the potential hostility between the younger and older man has already been negotiated in the forest in act 2, scene 7, a negotiation that results in the formation of an idealized male alliance. Rosalind submits not only to two individual men but also to the patriarchal society that they embody. Patriarchy is not a slogan smuggled in from the twentieth century and imposed on the play but an exact term for the social structure that close reading reveals within the play.

II

We are apt to assume that the green world is more free than it actually is. In the case of *As You Like It,* the green world cannot be interpreted as a space apart where a youthful rebellion finds a refuge from the older generation. The forest of Arden includes a strong parental presence: Duke Senior's is the first voice we hear there. Moreover, the green world has a clear political structure. Freed from the constraints of courtly decorum, Duke Senior can afford to address his companions as "brothers" (2.1.1), but he nonetheless retains a fatherly command. Fraternal spirit is not equivalent to democracy, as is clarified when the duke dispenses favor on a hierarchical basis: "Shall share the good of our returned fortune, / According to the measure of their states" (5.4.174–75).

Although interpretations of *As You Like It* often stress youthful love, we should not neglect the paternal context in which the love occurs. Both Rosalind and Orlando acknowledge Duke Senior. Rosalind is aware, as she finds herself attracted to Orlando, that "My father lov'd Sir Rowland [Orlando's father] as his soul" (1.2.235) and hence that her affection is not incompatible with family approval. Orlando, for his part, does not go forward in pursuit of love until after he has become friends with Duke Senior. Rosalind and Orlando approach the forest in strikingly different ways. Rosalind's mission is love. Upon entering the forest, she discovers there the love "passion" she has brought with her: "Alas, poor shepherd, searching of thy wound, / I have by hard adventure found mine own" (2.4.44–45). Orlando, by contrast, has two projects (though he does not consciously formulate them) to complete in the forest: the first is his quest to reestablish the broken connection with his father's legacy; the second is the quest for Rosalind. The sequence of these projects is an indication of priority. Orlando's outburst—"But heavenly Rosalind!" (1.2.289)—is not picked up again until he opens act 3, scene 2, with his love poem. The interim is reserved for his other, patriarchal business.

In the first scene of the play, Orlando makes it clear, in a melodramatic but nonetheless poignant way, that he derives his sense of identity from his dead father, an identity that is not yet fulfilled. In protesting against his older brother's mistreatment, Orlando asserts the paternal bond: "The spirit of my father grows strong in me, and I will no longer endure it" (1.1.70–71). His first step toward recovery of the connection with his lost father is the demolition of Charles the wrestler: "How dost thou, Charles?" / "He cannot speak, my lord" (1.2.219–20). This victory earns Orlando the right to proclaim his father's name as his own:

> DUKE FREDERICK: What is thy name, young man?
> ORLANDO: Orlando, my liege, the youngest son of Sir Rowland de Boys.
>
> .   .   .   .
>
> I am more proud to be Sir Rowland's son.
>
> (ll. 221–22, 232)

Frederick's negative reaction to Orlando's statement of identity confirms the concept of heritage being evoked here: "Thou shouldst have better pleas'd me with this deed / Hadst thou descended from another house" (ll. 227–28). The significance of the wrestling match is that

Orlando has undergone a traditional male rite of passage, providing an established channel for the violence he has previously expressed by collaring Oliver in the opening scene. Yet aggression is the epitome of a rigid masculinity that Shakespeare characteristically condemns as too narrow a basis for identity. Orlando's aggressiveness is instantly rendered inappropriate by his falling in love. Moreover, his recourse to violence simply mirrors the technique of the tyrannical Duke Frederick. As it turns out, Orlando must give up violence in order to meet the "good father."

While Rosalind's confidante Celia provides the opportunity to talk about love, Orlando is accompanied by Adam, who serves a very different function since he is a living link to Orlando's father. The paternal inheritance blocked by Oliver is received indirectly from Adam when he offers the money "I sav'd under your father, / Which I did store to be my foster-nurse" (2.3.39–40). The motif of nurturance implied by the "foster-nurse" image is continued as Orlando, through Adam's sudden collapse from lack of food, is led to Duke Senior's pastoral banquet. Treating this new situation as another trial of "the strength of my youth," Orlando imagines an all-or-nothing "adventure" (1.2.172, 177) similar to the wrestling match: "If this uncouth forest yield any thing savage, I will either be food for it, or bring it for food to thee" (2.6.6–8). In act 2, scene 7, he enters with drawn sword. Unexpectedly finding a benevolent father figure, Orlando effects as gracefully as possible a transition from toughness to tenderness: "Let gentleness my strong enforcement be, / In the which hope I blush, and hide my sword" (ll. 118–19). This display of nonviolence is the precondition for Orlando's recovery of patriarchal lineage. Duke Senior aids this recovery by his recognition of the father's reflection in the son and by his declaration of his own loving connection with Orlando's father. This transaction concludes the scene:

> If that you were the good Sir Rowland's son,
> As you have whisper'd faithfully you were,
> And as mine eye doth his effigies witness
> Most truly limn'd and living in your face,
> Be truly welcome hither. I am the Duke
> That lov'd your father.
>
> (ll. 191–96)

The confirmation of Orlando's identity has the effect of a ritual blessing that makes this particular father-son relation the basis

for social cohesion in general. There is much virtue in Orlando's
"If":

> ORLANDO: If ever you have look'd on better days,
>   If ever been where bells have knoll'd to church,
>   If ever sate at any good man's feast,
>   If ever from your eyelids wip'd a tear,
>   And know what 'tis to pity, and be pitied.
> DUKE SENIOR: True is it that we have seen better days,
>   And have with holy bell been knoll'd to church,
>   And sat at good men's feasts, and wip'd our eyes
>   Of drops that sacred pity hath engend'red.
>   (2.7.113–17, 120–23)

The liturgy of male utopia, ruthlessly undercut in *Love's Labor's Lost,* is
here allowed to stand. Virgilian piety, founded on ideal father-son
relations and evoked visually when, like Aeneas with Anchises, Orlando carries Adam on his back, can achieve what Navarre's academe
with its spurious abstinence could not. Orlando's heroic language as he
goes off to rescue Adam is as clumsy as any he uses in the poems to
Rosalind, but whereas the play pokes fun at the love poetry, the
expression of duty to Adam is not subject to irony: "Then but forbear
your food a little while, / Whiles, like a doe, I go to find my fawn, /
And give it food" (ll. 127–29). We are invited simply to accept the
doe-fawn metaphor that Orlando invokes for his obligation to recipro-
cate Adam's "pure love" (l. 131).

Just as there is an unlimited supply of food in this scene, so there
seems to be more than enough "pure love" to go around, Jaques
excepted. Love is expressed in terms of food, and men gladly take on
nurturant roles. Duke Senior's abundant provision of food and of
"gentleness" creates an image of a self-sustaining patriarchial system.
The men take over the traditional female prerogative of maternal
nurturance, negatively defined by Jaques: "At first the infant, / Mewling
and puking in the nurse's arms" (2.7.143–44). Such discomfort has
been purged from the men's nurturance as it is dramatized in this
scene, which thus offers a new perspective on Duke Senior's very first
speech in the play. We now see that it is the male feast, not the biting
winter wind, that "feelingly persuades me what I am" (2.1.11). "Sweet
are the uses of adversity" because, as Orlando discovers, adversity
disappears when men's "gentleness" prevails, "translating the stubbornness of fortune / Into so quiet and sweet a style" (ll. 12, 19–20).

This sweetness explains why "loving lords have put themselves into voluntary exile" with the duke and why "many young gentlemen flock to him every day" (1.1.101–2, 117).

The idealized male enclave founded on "sacred pity" in act 2, scene 7, is not an isolated incident. The power of male pity extends beyond this scene to include the evil Oliver, who is threatened by a symbol of maternal nurturance made hostile by depletion: "A lioness, with udders all drawn dry" (4.3.114) and "the suck'd and hungry lioness" (l. 126). The motif of eating here creates a negative image that might disturb the comfortable pastoral banquet, but the lioness's intrusion is quickly ended. Responding with a kindness that can be traced back to his meeting with Duke Senior, Orlando rescues his brother: "But kindness, nobler ever than revenge, / And nature, stronger than his just occasion, / Made him give battle to the lioness" (ll. 128–30). Oliver's oral fulfillment follows: "my conversion / So sweetly tastes" (136–37). The tears "that sacred pity hath engend'red" (2.7.123) are reiterated by the brothers' reconciliation—"Tears our recountments had most kindly bath'd" (4.3.140)—and their reunion confirmed by a recapitulation of the banquet scene: "he led me to the gentle Duke, / Who gave me fresh array and entertainment, / Committing me unto my brother's love" (142–44). Again the pattern of male reconciliation preceding love for women is seen in Oliver's confession of his desire to marry Celia (5.2.1–14) coming after his admission to the brotherhood.

The male community of act 2, scene 7, is also vindicated by the restoration of patriarchal normalcy in the play's final scene. In the end, as Rosalind's powers are fading, the relationship between Duke Senior and Orlando is reasserted and completed as the duke announces the inheritance to which marriage entitles Orlando: "A land itself at large, a potent dukedom" (5.4.169). Like the "huswife Fortune" who "doth most mistake in her gifts to women" (1.2.31–32, 36), Rosalind plays her part by rehearsing the men in their political roles:

> ROSALIND: You say, if I bring in your Rosalind,
>   You will bestow her on Orlando here?
> DUKE SENIOR: That would I, had I kingdoms to give with her.
> ROSALIND: And you say you will have her, when I bring her.
> ORLANDO: That would I, were I of all kingdoms king.
>
>   (5.4.6–10)

The reference the two men make to kingdoms is shortly to be fulfilled, but this bounty is beyond Rosalind's power to give. For it is not her magic that produces the surprise entrance of Jaques de Boys with the news of Duke Senior's restoration. In completing the de Boys family reunion, the middle brother's appearance reverses the emblematic fate of the three sons destroyed by Charles the wrestler: "Yonder they lie, the poor old man, their father, making such pitiful dole over them that all the beholders take his part with weeping" (1.2.129–32). The image of three de Boys sons reestablishes the proper generational sequence, ensuring continuity.

III

C. L. Barber has shown that the "Saturnalian Pattern" that gives structure to festive comedy is intrinsically conservative since it involves only "a temporary license, a 'misrule' which implied rule." But in *As You Like It* the conservatism of comic form does not affect all characters equally. In the liberal opening out into the forest of Arden, both men and women are permitted an expansion of sexual identity that transcends restrictive gender roles. Just as Rosalind gains access to the traditional masculine attributes of strength and control through her costume, so Orlando gains access to the traditional female attributes of compassion and nurturance. However, the conservative countermovement built into comic strategy applies exclusively to Rosalind. Her possession of the male costume and of the power it symbolizes is only temporary. But Orlando does not have to give up the emotional enlargement he has experienced in the forest. Discussions of androgyny in *As You Like It* usually focus on Rosalind whereas in fact it is the men rather than the women who are the lasting beneficiaries of androgyny. It is Orlando, not Rosalind, who achieves a synthesis of attributes traditionally labeled masculine and feminine when he combines compassion and aggression in rescuing his brother from the lioness.

This selective androgyny demands an ambivalent response: it is a humanizing force for the men, yet it is based on the assumption that men have power over women. Because androgyny is available only to men, we are left with a paradoxical compatibility of androgyny with patriarchy, that is, benevolent patriarchy. In talking about male power in *As You Like It,* we must distinguish between two forms of patriarchy. The first and most obvious is the harsh, mean-spirited version represented by Oliver, who abuses primogeniture, and by Duke Frederick, who after usurping power holds on to it by arbitrary acts of suppression. Driven by greed, envy, suspicion, and power for power's sake, neither man can explain his actions. In an ironic demonstration of the consuming nature of evil, Duke Frederick expends his final rage against Oliver, who honestly protests: "I never lov'd my brother in my life" (3.1.14). In contrast to good men, bad men are incapable of forming alliances. Since Frederick's acts of banishment have now depopulated the court, he himself must enter the forest in order to seek the enemies so necessary to his existence (5.4.154–58). But of course this patriarchal tyranny is a caricature and therefore harmless. Oliver and Frederick are exaggerated fairy-tale villains whose hardened characters are unable to withstand the wholesome atmosphere of the forest and instantly dissolve (4.3.135–37; 5.4.159–65). The second, more serious version of patriarchy is the political structure headed by Duke Senior. To describe it, we seek adjectives like "benevolent," "humane," and "civilized." Yet we cannot leave it at that. A benevolent patriarchy still requires women to be subordinate, and Rosalind's final performance is her enactment of this subordination.

We can now summarize the difference between the conclusions of *Love's Labor's Lost* and *As You Like It*. In order to assess the sense of an ending, we must take into account the perspective of sexual politics and correlate formal harmony or disharmony with patriarchal stability or instability. Unlike Rosalind, the women in *Love's Labor's Lost* do not give up their independence. The sudden announcement of the death of the princess's father partially restrains her wit. But this news is a *pater ex machina* attempt to even the score and to equalize the situation between the men and the women because nothing has emerged organically within the play to challenge the women's predominance. The revelation that the "decrepit, sick and bedred" father (1.1.138) has died is not an effective assertion of his presence but, on the contrary, advertises his weakness. The princess submits to the "new-sad soul" (5.2.731) that mourning requires, but this provides the excuse for going on to reject the suitors as she has all along. Her essential power remains intact, whereas patriarchal authority is presented as weak or nonexistent. The death of the invalid father has a sobering impact because it mirrors the vacuum created by the four lords' powerlessness within the play. There is no relief from the fear that dominant women inspire in a patriarchal sensibility, and this continuing tension contributes to the uneasiness at the play's end.

Like the princess, Rosalind confronts her father in the final scene. But in her case paternal power is vigorously represented by Duke Senior and by the line of patriarchal authority established when Senior makes Orlando his heir. Festive celebration is now possible because a dependable, that is, patriarchal, social order is securely in place. It is Duke Senior's voice that legitimates the festive closure: "Play, music, and you brides and bridegrooms all, / With measure heap'd in joy, to th' measures fall" (5.4.178–79). Orlando benefits from this social structure because, in contrast to the lords of *Love's Labor's Lost,* he has a solid political resource to offset the liability of a poetic convention that dictates male subservience. *As You Like It* achieves marital closure not by eliminating male ties but rather by strengthening them.

A further phasing out of Rosalind occurs in the Epilogue when it is revealed that she is male: "If I were a woman I would kiss as many of you as had beards that pleas'd me" (18–19). This explicit breaking of theatrical illusion forces us to reckon with the fact of an all-male cast. The boy-actor convention makes it possible for males to explore the female other (I use the term *other* here in the sense given by Simone de Beauvoir in *The Second Sex* of woman as the other). Vicariously taking on the female role enables male spectators to make an experimental contact with what otherwise might remain unknown, forbidden territory. Fear of women can be encountered in the relatively safe environment of the theater, acted out, controlled (when it can be controlled as in *As You Like It*), and overcome. A further twist of logic defuses and reduces the threat of female power: Rosalind is no one to be frightened of since, as the Epilogue insists, she is male after all; she is only a boy and clearly subordinate to men in the hierarchy of things.

The convention of males playing female roles gives men the opportunity to imagine sex-role fluidity and flexibility. Built into the conditions of performance is the potential for male acknowledgment of a "feminine self" and thus for male transcendence of a narrow masculinity. In the particular case of *As You Like It,* the all-male cast provides a theatrical counterpart for the male community at Duke Senior's banquet in act 2, scene 7. This theatrical dimension reinforces the conservative effect of male androgyny within the play. Acknowledgment of the feminine within the male is one thing, the acknowledgment of individual women another: the latter does not automatically follow from the former. In the boy-actor motif, woman is a metaphor for the male discovery of the feminine within himself, of those qualities suppressed by a masculinity strictly defined as aggressiveness. Once the tenor of the metaphor has been attained, the vehicle can be discarded—just as Rosalind is discarded. The sense of the patriarchal ending in *As You Like It* is that male androgyny is affirmed whereas female "liberty" in the person of Rosalind is curtailed.

There is, finally, a studied ambiguity about heterosexual versus homoerotic feeling the play, Shakespeare allowing himself to have it both ways. The Epilogue is heterosexual in its bringing together of men and women: "and I charge you, O men, for the love you bear to women (as I perceive by your simp'ring, none of you hates them), that between you and the women the play may please" (ll. 14–17). The "simp'ring" attributed to men in their response to women is evoked in a good-natured jocular spirit; yet the tone conveys discomfort as well. In revealing the self-sufficient male company, the Epilogue also offers the counterimage of male bonds based on the exclusion of women.

Though he is shown hanging love poems on trees only after achieving atonement with Rosalind's father, Orlando never tries, like the lords of *Love's Labor's Lost,* to avoid women. The social structure of *As You Like It,* in which political power is vested in male bonds, can include heterosexual love because marriage becomes a way of incorporating women since Rosalind is complicit in her assimilation by patriarchal institutions. However, in spite of the disarming of Rosalind, resistance to women remains. It is as though asserting the priority of relations between men over relations between men and women is not enough, as though a fall-back position is needed. The Epilogue is, in effect, a second ending that provides further security against women by preserving on stage the image of male ties in their pure form with women absent. Not only are women to be subordinate; they can, if necessary, be imagined as nonexistent. Rosalind's art does not, as is sometimes suggested, coincide with Shakespeare's: Shakespeare uses his art to take away Rosalind's female identity and thereby upstages her claim to magic power.

We can see the privileged status accorded to male bonds by comparing Shakespeare's treatment of same-sex relations for men and for women. Men originally divided are reunited as in the instance of Oliver and Orlando, but women undergo the reverse process. Rosalind and Celia are initially inseparable: "never two ladies lov'd as they do" (1.1.112); "whose loves / Are dearer than the natural bond of sisters" (1.2.275–76); "And whereso'er we went, like Juno's swans, / Still we went coupled and inseparable" (1.3.75–76); and "thou and I am one. / Shall we be sund'red? shall we part, sweet girl? / No, let my father seek another heir" (ll. 97–99). Yet the effect of the play is to separate them by transferring their allegiance to husbands. Celia ceases to be a speaking character at the end of act 4, her silence coinciding with her new role as fiancée. The danger of female bonding is illustrated when Shakespeare diminishes Rosalind's absolute control by mischievously confronting her with the unanticipated embarrassment of Phebe's love for her. Rosalind is of course allowed to devise an escape from the pressure of this undesirable entanglement, but it is made clear in the process that such ardor is taboo and that the authorized defense against it is marriage. "And so am I for no woman," Rosalind insists (5.2.88). A comparable prohibition is not announced against male friendship.

In conclusion, we must ask: what is Shakespeare's relation to the sexual politics of *As You Like It?* Is he taking an ironic and critical stance toward the patriarchal solution of his characters, or is he heavily invested in this solution himself? I think there are limits to Shakespeare's critical awareness in this play. The sudden conversions of Oliver and Duke Frederick have a fairy-tale quality that Shakespeare clearly intends as an aspect of the wish fulfillment to which he calls attention in the play's title. Similarly, Jaques's commentary in the final scene is a deliberate foil to the neatness of the ending that allows Shakespeare as well as Jaques a modicum of distance. However, in fundamental respects Shakespeare appears to be implicated in the fantasy he has created for his characters.

As You Like It enacts two rites of which Shakespeare did not avail himself in *Love's Labor's Lost.* First, Shakespeare has the social structure ultimately contain female energy as he did not in *Love's Labor's Lost.* We have too easily accepted the formulation that says that Shakespeare in the mature history plays concentrates on masculine development whereas in the mature festive comedies he gives women their due by allowing them to play the central role. *As You Like It* is primarily a defensive action against female power rather than a celebration of it. Second, Shakespeare portrays an ideal male community based on "sacred pity." This idealized vision of relationships between men can be seen as sentimental and unrealistic, but in contrast to his undercutting of academe in *Love's Labor's Lost,* Shakespeare is here thoroughly engaged and endorses the idealization. These two elements—female vitality kept manageable and male power kept loving—provided a resolution that at this particular moment was "As Shakespeare Liked It."

Mixed Gender, Mixed Genre in Shakespeare's *As You Like It*

Barbara J. Bono

Does Shakespeare's preoccupation, especially in the comedies, with strong female characters and an underlying complex of "feminine" concerns—sexuality and familial and domestic life—provide evidence for what Juliet Dusinberre calls a "feminism of Shakespeare's time"? Or does the same evidence indicate male projections of what women must be, what Madelon Gohlke terms a "matriarchal substratum or subtext within the patriarchal text" that "is not feminist," but rather "provide[s] a rationale for the structure of male dominance"? Put more generally, does the literature and social practice of the early modern period exhibit, as Stephen Greenblatt and Natalie Zemon Davis suggest, a theatricality, a ready embrace of role playing and social inversion, that nonetheless functions most often to test and strengthen traditional authority? And if, with Davis and, more tentatively, Greenblatt, we wish to argue that the subversion occasionally escapes its cultural containment, how does this escape occur, and in what does it, or our latter-day perception of it, consist? In this essay I seek to erect a framework of contemporary feminist theory around a traditional genre-based analysis of the heroic, romantic, and pastoral strains in Shakespeare's *As You Like It* in order to conjure a complex response to these questions.

Recently Nancy Chodorow has offered a powerful and influential

From *Renaissance Genres: Essays on Theory, History, and Interpretation,* edited by Barbara Kiefer Lewalski. © 1986 by the President and Fellows of Harvard College. Harvard University Press, 1986.

new model for psychoanalysis and the sociology of gender that seems very useful for analyzing the representation of gender in literature as well. In an object-relations account of identity formation that stresses the temporal primacy of the mother, Chodorow presses her analysis back beyond the oedipal phase to the preoedipal phase, significantly revising Freud's classic accounts of both masculinity and femininity.

Freud privileges the male sex in his account of gender identity, speaking of the oedipal castration fear of the boy child and the penis envy of the girl child. But by placing the mother as socializer at the heart of her account, Chodorow characterizes gender and sexual differentiation not "as presence or absence of masculinity and the male genital" but as "two different presences." The male child defines himself in a tension-fraught opposition to his potentially engulfing mother, while the female child has the more complex and extended, if less extreme, task of simultaneously affirming a gender identity with the mother and an individual differentiation from her. A girl child's "penis envy" is, then, not a recognition of a primary lack but a secondary, defensive reaction against maternal power and an attempted appropriation of what is seen as greater masculine autonomy from it. Chodorow argues that the events of the oedipal period must be understood against this preoedipal background that is itself more centrally a social than a biological experience: "In fact, what occurs for both sexes during the oedipal period is a product of this knowledge about gender and its social and familial significance, rather than the reverse (as the psychoanalytic accounts have it).

The strengths of Chodorow's clinically documented and tenaciously argued model seem to me many. Her stress on the early, preconscious psychological formation of these patterns in interaction with a female mother who is primary caretaker explains the seeming universality, rootedness, and strong elements of complicity in those arrangements through which women become the "second sex." Although the responsibility has often been diffused or configured somewhat differently, primary female mothering has been a cultural and historical constant. However, it need not be an inevitability. Chodorow's theory is genuinely anthropological and sociological in denying biological determinism and in noting considerable differences in the social practice of mothering, and it shares with thinkers like Dorothy Dinnerstein a revolutionary feminist belief in the possibility of change in our sexual arrangements based on changing the sexual division of labor into shared parenting.

It also contains an embryonic historical dimension, for Chodorow notes that the emphasis on the single female mother has altered over time. She comments especially on the effects of modern capitalism in widening the sexual division of labor by separating home and workplace and institutionalizing within the workplace a division between largely female service occupations and the ideal of a male worker detached from prior community, eager to succeed, and highly malleable to organizational needs. Certain features of this analysis seem relevant to the early modern period in England, during the rise of capitalism—the period when Shakespeare's plays were written. Then men, often no longer owners or caretakers of land in a feudal system, were sent out early for education or apprenticeship and took up entrepreneurial schemes in court and city, while patriarchal values kept women even more closely tied to the work of childbearing and motherhood.

Coppélia Kahn has demonstrated the applicability of Chodorow's theory of gender formation to the representation of male personality in Shakespeare's plays, particularly *King Lear*. Arguing that Lear's unconscious male fear of maternal power is displaced into metaphoric expression, Kahn instances his loathing of his "pelican daughters" and his shame at his own woman's tears and "female" hysteria (the "climbing mother," the disorder of the wandering womb). She might also have added the most inclusive metaphoric expression in the play of this threatening female power, the goddess-Mother Nature whom Edmund invokes to "stand up for bastards," and who proves Lear and his followers not ague-proof. The implication of this sexual metaphorization of landscape is that pastoral and anti-pastoral—"soft" and "hard" primitivism—may figure the opposite sides of the male crisis of individuation from the mother—nurturance or antipathy.

Kahn's methodological tactic supports Louis Montrose's excellent sociological reading of that pastoral play, *As You Like It*. Focusing explicitly on the historically sensitive oedipal situation of brothers' rivalry over a paternal inheritance, Montrose rightly restores balance to the interpretation of the play by dwelling on the very engaging plot of Orlando's rise that frames Rosalind's androgynous disguising. He devotes the penultimate section of his essay on "the complex interrelationship of brothers, fathers, and sons in *As You Like It*" to a suggestive discussion of Rosalind and of the play's strategies for containment of the feminine. In Montrose's shrewd formulation, "The 'feminism' of Shakespearean comedy seems to me more ambivalent in tone and more ironic in form than such critics [those infatuated with Rosalind's exuberance] have wanted to believe. Kahn's work suggests that from a male point of view both Rosalind and Arden are initially threatening but eventually beneficent manifestations of a nonfeminist maternal subtext. It is possible, then, that in Shakespeare's works both the explicitly threatening women of the tragedies and the seemingly benevolent women of the comedies operate within a "universe of masculinist assumptions" about the nature of women.

Yet Chodorow's model would also argue for a positive female identity, although one severely handicapped by the perception of itself as culturally secondary. Kahn and Montrose do not inquire whether Shakespearean drama can plausibly represent this point of view, and if so, whether that drama can provide us with any tool for dislodging "the universe of masculinist assumptions" in which it is embedded. In what follows I would like to sketch both Orlando's and Rosalind's roles in the play on the basis of Chodorow's model for the formation of gender identity. I shall argue that the patriarchal, oedipal crisis of the first act of the play is displaced back onto its preoedipal ground in the nature of the forest of Arden—that place named suggestively after Shakespeare's own mother, Mary Arden, and the forest near his birthplace at Stratford-on-Avon. There the play can represent both the male struggle for identity and a female "double-voiced" discourse—Elaine Showalter's term for one that simultaneously acknowledges its dependence on the male and implies its own unique positive value—within it.

For this Shakespeare employs, of course, not a modern psychoanalytic or sociological vocabulary, but his period's vocabulary of genre, set within the consciously experimental frame of the mixed genre of pastoral. Orlando's masculine heroic quest, couched simultaneously in the language of biblical typology and classical epic, is resolved within Arden's "sweet style." There Rosalind, fully acting out romance's conventions of disguise, transforms the social perception of woman from the Petrarchan conventions that both idealize and degrade them to a new convention of companionate marriage. Unlike Orlando's simpler quest, Rosalind's "double-voiced" discourse, criticizing the subject of which she is a part, can thus offer a method for cultural change. She performs *within* the text the critical task feminists today must perform *toward the text as a whole.* As Madelon Gohlke says, "For a feminist critic to deconstruct this discourse is simultaneously to recognize her own historicity and to engage in the process of dislocation of the unconscious by which she begins to affirm her own reality."

But only begins. Rosalind's deconstructive efforts within her own text are one such beginning—a method, not an ideal end. Ironically, she resubordinates herself through marriage to masculine hierarchy, giving herself to her father to be given to her husband, and thus serves the socially conservative purpose of Shakespearean romantic comedy. And "she," of course, acts out a fiction of femininity on an exclusively male stage, her part played by a boy. The representation of women has, more often than not, functioned this way in literature, as in life—as an accommodating device within the dominant fictions of male identity.

Thus far I have emphasized Rosalind's critical role within the text and her eventual surrender of it. Nonetheless, the interaction in *As You Like It* between masculine heroic discourse and feminine romantic "double-voiced" discourse, which it is the burden of this essay to document, forms the dramatic "inside" to a metadramatic context or "outside" of more pure interpretative possibility. Rosalind's disguise, initially the most striking convention of romance implausibility in this text that is so largely structured like an "old tale" (1.2.120), ultimately functions to create new possibilities for it. Her mutable action most fully demonstrates Touchstone's peacemaking "If" (5.4.97–103); Ganymede—the lovely boy whose rapture connected earth and heaven— predicates Hymen, the god of marriage who will "atone" all the elements of the play. In this play romance sustains the constructive, as well as the critical, aspects of pastoral. Arden and the audience addressed in the "Epilogue" function as the complementary en- vironments of the play. Although, looking ahead to *Lear,* I shall characterize the pastoral environment of Arden as a sometimes harsh, sometimes nurturing "Mother Nature"; it is also, as Amiens hints to the Duke, a theater for literary and social criticism and change. For the culturally belated urban artists of the Renaissance, pastoral, which in theory promised a return to origins and a poetic apprentice- ship, in practice often presented itself as a field for heightened reflexivity, itself criticizing the subject—the larger culture—of which it formed a part. The "Epilogue" to *As You Like It* freely acknow- ledges affect as in part constituting the meaning of a work of art: although we may never know what Shakespeare's audience made of the actor-playing-Rosalind's final address, we are licensed to make of it what pleases. At the close of this essay I shall offer a few tentative speculations on why Shakespeare himself, in his later career, made dif- ficult or surrendered this "poco tempo silvano," this play-space of pastoral. But within *As You Like It,* at least, we and the forest are the final judges.

In Shakespeare's *As You Like It* both Duke Senior and Orlando are victims of parricidal rage. The anger of Orlando's brother Oliver is given biblical and classical archetypal overtones as their old family retainer Adam, a representative of the Golden Age "When service sweat for duty, not for meed" (2.3.58), stands in place of their father to bemoan the loss of original "accord" and to denounce Oliver, that Cain figure, who has made "this house . . . but a butchery" (1.1.64; 2.3.27). Shakespeare heightens the at once fairy-tale and all-too-contemporary figure of the impoverished younger brother into an image of paradise lost, where the rising spirit of one's father threatens to turn into rankling bitterness.

Orlando does not seek the patrimony. He desires only his "poor allottery" of "but poor a thousand crowns" (1.1.73; 1.1.2–3) and his due "breeding" in gentility. Ironically, he has only his physical strength, his wrestler's skill, to prove these largely immaterial claims, and even his victory over Charles is immediately frustrated by Duke Frederick's antipathy. As with Chodorow's oedipally fraught male child, these problems in the patriarchy open a greater void in his identity, a potential regression to a threatening maternal subtext. Orlando fears that his growth may prove, as Oliver says, "rank" ([compare] 1.1.13 with 1.1.85–86). In the wrestling scene Charles taunts him with being, like Antaeus, "desirous to lie with his mother earth" (1.2.201). Although Orlando at first inverts the allusion by defeating Charles as the moral Hercules defeated Antaeus, he then assimilates some of its force when, in a "modest" displacement of Charles's incestuous image, he finds himself violently in love with Rosalind. His formerly dignified speech before Rosalind is now shattered as the deepest dimension of his insecurity, his lack of good breeding, surfaces ([compare] 1.2.165–93 and 245–60), and he fears exile in an inhospitable nature where he might have to beg, or, like Tom Jones, fall in with robbers (1.1.75; 2.3.31–35).

When Orlando flees to the forest, he expects to encounter savagery. Instead, this young man struggling for gentility—"inland bred" (2.7.96)—meets not brigands but a kindly, paternal, philosophic ruler, the exiled Duke: "Sit down and feed, and welcome to our table" (2.7.105). Shakespeare compresses in this brief exchange the ancient ideal of hospitality, those guest-rites most fully performed in the offering of a meal, the contemplative counterweight to epic's celebra-

tion of martial deeds and heroic adventure. And as with Odysseus at
Alcinous's house or Aeneas at Dido's banquet, the gesture releases
Orlando's pent-up memory and social desire. His deeply moving lit-
any of the ceremonies of civilization is ritually echoed by the Duke:

> True is it that we have seen better days,
> And have with holy bell been knoll'd to church,
> And sat at good men's feasts, and wip'd our eyes
> Of drops that sacred pity hath engend'red;
> And therefore sit you down in gentleness,
> And take upon command what help we have
> That to your wanting may be minist'red.
>
> (2.7.120–26)

The text expands momentarily into a calm reflective pool of noble
pity—"sunt lacrimae rerum et mentem mortalia tangunt" ("here, too,
there are tears for misfortune and mortal sorrows touch the heart,"
Aeneid, 1.462). A moment later Orlando visually contradicts Jaques's
vivid but reductionistic image of the "seven ages of man" by entering
with the frail old Adam, quite possibly borne on his shoulders, and
thereby evoking that classical image of *pietas,* Aeneas carrying his father
Anchises from burning Troy (2.7.139–68). Then, even while Amiens
sings of man's ingratitude, the Duke discovers that Orlando is his
beloved "good Sir Rowland's son" (2.7.191–92) and welcomes him to
his new society.

The Duke's masculine governing identity has not been violently
dislocated by exile. Unlike Lear, who feels the "climbing mother,"
gives way to women's tears, and, in a sharply discontinuous action
marked by disjoint, raving speech, exposes himself to the raging
elements, Duke Senior exercises seemingly benign verbal control over
his environment. The balanced blank verse of his first speech moves to
contain the sharp sensuous apprehension of difference: "the icy fang /
And churlish chiding of the winter's wind, / Which . . . bites and
blows upon my body" is literally bracketed by his declaration that
"Here feel we *not* the penalty of Adam" and his smiling philosophic
conclusion (2.1.5–17, emphasis mine). The Duke tries to surround the
threatening nature that had opened up with the failure of the patriarchy
in the first act, controlling it so that Orlando, and to a large extent we,
now experience it as the playfulness of Rosalind, rather than the
threat of unnurturing and devouring mother. His "kindly," "sweet"
stylization—the words resonate with the high philosophic seriousness

of the *dolce stil nuovo* and its ideals of gentility—now permits the growth of Orlando's romantic art.

Chodorow speaks of boys as having to "define themselves as more separate and distinct [from the mother], with a greater sense of rigid ego boundaries and differentiation," and thus resolving their oedipal crisis more rapidly, extremely, and definitively than girls. The resolution takes the form of "identification with his father . . . the superiority of masculine identification and prerogatives over feminine" (in Freud's more extreme language, "What we have come to consider the normal male contempt for women"), and the eventual displacement of his primary love for his mother onto an appropriate heterosexual love object. Orlando, after initial conflict with paternal figures—his older brother and Duke Frederick—which nearly culminates in archetypal tragedy, experiences nature as harshly threatening. He is saved from its ravages by a kindly father figure who thus metaphorically restores the archetypal line of paternal descent. With the confidence of that masculine relatedness he is able to play seriously at the civilized game of love without threatening his basic male heroic identity. Then Rosalind-as-Ganymede can work to refine his personality while being herself ultimately contained by an overt masculinist sexual ideology.

Meanwhile, similar social problems unfold differently in an aristocratic women's world. Instead of Orlando's importunate strivings, Rosalind at court displays a more diffuse melancholy, partially relieved by feminine confidences—Chodorow's female "self in relationship." Rosalind's musings about the precarious social position of women in love—"[Fortune] the bountiful blind woman doth most mistake in her gifts to women" (1.2.35–36)—suggest that the Duke's exile, deeply felt though it is, is less important than her problematic femininity, especially without his protection. And the desultory and slightly forced nature of the talk portrays the extreme constraints on women's expression in such a setting. Even Touchstone's flat joke about the pancakes must be triggered by a reminder of their feminine lack of a beard (1.2.60–80)! Against this sense of inferiority and vulnerability the young women here have only ready wit.

Exiled by her tyrannous uncle, Rosalind assumes masculine disguise as a safeguard against female vulnerability in a threatening male world. Once she is safely installed in her cottage in Arden, however, there is in theory no need for her to maintain that role. Indeed, once she hears from Celia that young Orlando, who at court "tripp'd up the wrastler's heels and your heart, both in an instant" (3.2.212–13), is in the forest poeticizing her praises, she immediately exclaims, "Alas the day, what shall I do with my doublet and hose?" (3.2.219–20), and bursts forth with a stereotypically female torrent of questions and effusions, ending with "Do you not know I am a woman? when I think, I must speak" (3.2.249–50). She seems on the verge of throwing off her masculine attire and becoming the Renaissance total woman: witty, perhaps, but ultimately compliant.

At this moment, however, Orlando and Jaques enter in conversation. They implicitly raise the issue of women's dependence on men that Rosalind's exile from the court has merely transferred from the political to the psychological sphere. Orlando's "pretty answers," the love commonplaces that Touchstone has already parodied (2.4.46–56; 3.2.100–112) and that Rosalind herself has criticized as "tedious" and having "more feet than the verses would bear" (3.2.155, 165–66), are now attacked by the satiric Jaques, "Monsieur Melancholy." Although Orlando, "Signior Love," holds his own in this comic agon, it is not at all clear from the women's point of view that his disagreement with Jaques is anything more than a battle of wits masking potentially violent sexual appetite. As Jaques accuses, Orlando may be tritely copying his "posies" out of the inscriptions inside goldsmiths' rings. More ominously, he may have "conn'd" the "rings" themselves from the goldsmiths' wives, where the connotations "con" = "pudendum" and "rings" = "vagina" suggest seduction. As Celia warns, if you drink in this type of discourse uncritically, you risk putting a "man in your belly" (3.2.204). Hearing this affected and subtly threatening exchange prompts Rosalind to keep her doublet and hose, and what is more, to use them in exactly the sort of "double-voiced" discourse that, according to Showalter, has always characterized the relationship of female to male culture: "I will speak to him like a saucy lackey, and under that habit play the knave with him" (3.2.295–97). That is, she will adopt the "habit"—the clothing and habitual ways—of the dominant male culture, including its view of women, even while skewing it "saucily" toward self-consciousness and criticism, and maintaining a part of herself hidden and inviolate.

Nancy Vickers, in a recent article on Petrarchism implies the defensive wisdom of this tactic. This tradition imagines a chaste, inaccessible, Dianalike woman as the object of the male speaker's love, engendering in him a narcissistically luxuriant range of contradictory emotions that further objectify her, retributively fragmenting her body. Shakespeare continually documents and criticizes this pathology, from

Romeo's bookish love for the chaste Rosalind, to Orsino's self-indulgent laments after the "cloistered" Olivia, to its *reductio ad absurdum* in Troilus's languishing after the parts of Cressida, soon to become nauseating "fragments, scraps, the bits and greasy relics / Of her o'er-eaten faith" (5.2.159–60). Within this self-generating fiction the only power that women seem to have is the defensive one of refusal, for then, at least, they may put off being consumed and discarded: as Cressida says: "Therefore this maxim out of love I teach: / Achievement is command; ungain'd beseech" (1.2.293–94). Orlando hymns a Dianalike Rosalind in a patently artificial language predicated on the Duke's philosophic sweet style; instead of finding "tongues in trees" (2.1.16), the eager new versifier vandalizes them: "these trees shall be my books, / And in their barks my thoughts I'll character" (3.2.5–6). Rosalind witnesses the hitherto uncultivated Orlando's burgeoning conventional love poetry, and by remaining a boy at first defensively distances herself from it.

But Rosalind ultimately accomplishes something more constructive through her pastoral disguise as Ganymede, that pretty boy beloved by Jove, alternately a figure of sexual degradation or of ecstasy. By self-consciously retaining her superficially plausible disguise as a girlish boy—that is, by seeming to "be" Ganymede offering to "play" Rosalind—Rosalind simultaneously offers Orlando a chance to test "the faith of . . . [his] love" (3.2.428) within the relatively nonthreatening limits of supposed male discourse about women, and attempts to exorcise her own fears about giving herself into such a discourse.

In doing so she illustrates the greater social burden borne by women, in line with Chodorow's contention that the oedipus complex develops "different forms of 'relational potential' in people of different genders" and that "Girls emerge from this period with a basis for 'empathy' built into their primary definition of self in a way that boys do not." Having suffered an oedipal crisis in the first act of the play because of the exile of her father and the opposition of Duke Frederick, Rosalind too is thrown back upon nature. Unlike Orlando, however, she does not experience this preoedipal nature as harshly threatening, nor does she require the immediate assurances of a restored father figure. Instead she arrives "weary" but resourceful; female ennervation in the court here translates into boyish pluck (2.4.1–8). As Chodorow says, "girls do not define themselves in terms of the denial of preoedipal relational modes to the same extent as do boys. Therefore, regression to these modes tends not to feel as much a basic threat to their ego."

Chodorow's careful characterization of "a relational complexity in feminine self-definition and personality which is not characteristic of masculine self-definition or personality" not only highlights the difference between Rosalind's and Orlando's reactions to Arden; it also helps explain why Rosalind/Ganymede behaves the way she/he does here. In Arden Rosalind discovers a female identity that will allow her to complete the difficult, triangulated resolution of a girl's typical oedipal crisis: differentiation from *and* continuity with the mother and transfer of affection from the father onto an appropriate heterosexual love object. She must act out her own involvement with this less threatening "Mother Nature" in a way that does not shatter Orlando's more fragile ego boundaries; having done so she may deliver herself to the restored patriarchy, giving herself to her father to be given by him in marriage to her husband.

Her interaction as Ganymede/Rosalind with Orlando thus functions from the male perspective as a form of accommodation and as a test. In the court Orlando had been tongue-tied before beautiful, young, aristocratic women; freed and newly confident in the forest he understandably blurts out clichés. Talk with an attractive boy about women can work to root and refine his discourse, as encounter with "the real thing" at this point could not. Orlando recovers his quietly dignified desire in conversation with Ganymede: "I am he that is so love-shak'd"; "I would not be cur'd"; "By the faith of my love" (3.2.367, 425, 428). Meanwhile, Rosalind/Ganymede tests "the faith of . . . [his] love" against the tradition of misogyny that the unrealistic idealism of Petrarchism could reinforce. As a young man supposedly educated by a sexually disillusioned and withdrawn "old religious uncle of mine" (3.2.344), she professes scepticism toward Orlando and cynicism toward women (3.2.369–71, 348–50), and in her succeeding therapy, proposing to cure love by counsel, she acts out for his benefit men's stereotypical expectations of women's fickleness and seeming cruelty

in this manner. He was to imagine me his love, his mistress; and I set him every day to woo me. At which time would I, being but a moonish youth, grieve, be effeminate, changeable, longing and liking, proud, fantastical, apish, shallow, inconstant, full of tears, full of smiles . . . that I drave my suitor from his mad humor of love to a living humor of madness, which was, to forswear the full stream of the world, and live in a nook merely monastic.

(3.2.407–12, 417–21)

In response to her trying poses, Orlando remains constant. The Orlando we see in the final act of the play is now appropriately sceptical of fanciful love at first sight and has painfully earned the "real" love he is given.

However, he does not develop a very much more sophisticated understanding of women's ambiguous position in the world. Throughout Rosalind's disguising, Orlando retains an essentially simple faith grounded in his newly secure identity in the Duke's service. He has an increasingly melancholy feeling that this interlude is just a game—that he may be wasting time—and he breaks off wooing to "attend the Duke at dinner" (4.1.180). Rosalind's action as Ganymede/Rosalind does not shock or void his identity in the way nature had earlier threatened to do; instead she leads him to revise his Petrarchan idealization of women—"The fair, the chaste, the unexpressive she" (3.2.10)—toward a desire for a chaste wife, and sets that desire within the dominant code for his male heroic identity.

Rosalind as Ganymede, however, transforms herself more thoroughly. As her words imply, she is not a dispassionate therapist: "Love is merely a madness, and I tell you, deserves as well a dark house and a whip as madmen do; and the reason why they are not so punish'd and cur'd is that *the lunacy is so ordinary that the whippers are in love too*" (3.2.400–404, emphasis mine). Critics have always commented on Rosalind's control of decorum while in disguise, but in a play written almost contemporaneously with *Hamlet* her "holiday humor" (4.1.69), like his "antic disposition," is as much used to exorcise her own fears about love as it is to criticize or educate her lover. Rosalind's control lies in standing outside of amatory convention, but it is her action within these conventions that carries her, almost imperceptibly, into the "magic" of creating a new, and within the value judgments of this play, more adequate convention of companionate marriage.

This becomes clear in her interaction with Silvius and Phebe. During a frustrating break in her play with Orlando—he is late for his appointment with her—she slips from her earlier facile and uncritical sympathy for Silvius's mooning "shepherd's passion" (2.4.60) to a desire to *do* something, to enter their amusingly static and artificial pastoral "pageant" and "prove a busy actor in their play" (3.4.47–59). What she does there, quite to her surprise, is to become the sexually ambiguous means—a boyish "ripe sister" (4.3.87)—through which their hopelessly stalemated and conventional Petrarchan attitudes are softened toward reciprocal love. Silvius, who has previously been an utter fool in love, running off stage (as Orlando later does for Rosalind) exclaiming "O Phebe, Phebe, Phebe!" (2.4.43), assumes a sober fidelity under Ganymede's rebuke; the disdainful Phebe, having now felt the pang of love for Ganymede, is at least sorry for "gentle" Silvius (3.5.85). When Rosalind dissolves her disguise at the end of the play, they have seen each other through her, and Phebe assures Silvius that "Thy faith my fancy to thee doth combine" (5.4.150).

Rosalind-as-Ganymede's action within Silvius and Phebe's play has double relevance for her action within her own. It makes explicit her androgynous power, even while it implies her own subliminal desire to give herself to Orlando. In her next scene with Orlando she fulfills her earlier plan (4.1), acting as she thinks men expect women to do, alternately Lady Disdain and the threateningly promiscuous dark lady of the sonnets. The vehemence and verve of her acting here argues that she is now doing this as much for her own sake as for Orlando's. It is necessary for her to misuse her sex, to soil her own nest, as Celia half-jokingly puts it (4.1.201–4), in order to hide the "woman's fear" (1.3.119) in her heart. She must act out her ambivalence toward her social inscription as woman in order to participate in male privilege. Yet she has just sharply criticized such behavior in Phebe, urging her to "thank heaven, fasting, for a good man's love" (3.5.58), and in 4.1 she becomes confident enough in Orlando's faithful replies to stage a mock marriage. Temporarily empowered *within* Petrarchan love conventions, she has worked her way through to surrendering them in favor of a provisional trust in her partially tested lover. The imaginative space provided by the forest can take her this far—to an imagined wedding.

It takes an intrusion from outside the forest and a resurgence of male heroic force to turn the imagined wedding into a real one. The Duke's "kindness" and Rosalind-as-Ganymede's "play" have allowed Orlando to become a moral rather than merely a physical Hercules (see the wrestling match and Rosalind's cry at 1.2.210), and thus also a type of Christ. Those inchoate energies which in the court could find expression only through wrestling Charles, in the forest focus on the picture of "A wretched ragged man, o'ergrown with hair" and menaced by a snake and a lioness (4.3.102–32). Suddenly Arden has grown threatening again, its postlapsarian state implied by the snake; its maternal peril implied by the Ovidian "suck'd and hungry lioness"; the masculine fear of return to nature emblematized as the supposed wild man. This threat presents itself to Orlando as a moral dilemma, for he recognizes the endangered man as his brother, his eldest brother, "that same brother . . . the most unnatural / That liv'd amongst men." The "old oak, whose boughs were moss'd with age / And high top bald with dry antiquity" and the "wretched ragged man, o'ergrown with hair" both suggest patriarchal and epic genealogy brought to the verge of savagery and decay by Oliver and Duke Frederick's actions: as Orlando earlier laments, "a rotten tree, / That cannot so much as a blossom yield" (2.3.63–64). The description builds to a climax that Shakespeare will repeat near the end of *The Tempest*. To Rosalind's anxious query, "But to Orlando: did he leave him there, / Food to the suck'd and hungry lioness?" the stranger, like Prospero to Ariel (*Temp.*, 5.1.24–28), replies:

> kindness, nobler ever than revenge,
> And nature, stronger than his just occasion,
> Made him give battle to the lioness,
> Who quickly fell before him.

Orlando redeems Eden, and the story bursts into present reality with all the force of its teller's awaking and sudden conversion to brotherly love: "in which hurtling / From miserable slumber *I* awaked" (emphasis mine).

The stranger is thus revealed as Orlando's eldest brother, Oliver. His conversion is emphasized by the dramatic introduction of the personal pronoun and the succeeding insistent play upon it (4.3.135–37). Oliver declares that his real identity surfaced from disguise through disguise; he states that his former unnaturalness has been "sweetly" transformed in the forest; he undergoes in a flash the experience of male bonding, of kinship, that his brother had found with the exiled Duke, to whose society Orlando now leads him (4.3.142–44).

The bloody napkin Oliver brings to Ganymede/Rosalind emblematizes the male adversarial experience of the world of nature. The sign of Orlando's wounding by the lioness, it intrudes the reality of death into Arden: *et in Arcadia ego*. Because of it Rosalind discovers how empathetically tied she is to Orlando: Oliver reports "he [Orlando] fainted, / And cried in fainting upon Rosalind," (4.3.148–49), and Ganymede also promptly swoons. She can now only lamely maintain her disguise; events have impelled her toward accepting this "reality," even with its implied threat to herself—for the "bloody napkin" will reappear in *Othello* as the strawberried handkerchief, a threatening emblem of the dangers of sexual consummation.

Things happen quickly after this. Orlando, now "estate[d]" with the patrimony by his grateful brother, readily gives consent to Oliver's marriage to Celia (5.2.1–15). The improbability of this marriage is satisfactorily glossed by Rosalind/Ganymede's witty "pair of stairs to marriage" speech (5.2.29–41), which at once raises our objections to the suddenness of it and reminds us that it is her own protracted negotiation with Orlando that predicates our conditional acceptance of this love at first sight. Rosalind is having increasing difficulty maintaining her disguise as Oliver and Orlando's words seem to cut closer and closer to her real identity. Pressured by Orlando's emotional urgency—"I can live no longer by thinking"—Rosalind/Ganymede declares, "I will weary you then no longer with idle talking" (5.2.50–52). Persuaded now by Orlando's "gesture" (5.2.62), which I take to be as much his heroic action in saving his brother as his fidelity within their love discourse, Ganymede promises to produce Rosalind to marry Orlando in truth tomorrow.

In the final act of *As You Like It* Rosalind seemingly surrenders the play. She gives herself to the Duke her father so that he may give her to Orlando (5.4.19-20, 116-18). She thus reminds us that their initial attraction to each other was as much through their fathers—the old Sir Rowland de Boys whom Duke Senior loved as his soul (1.2.235–39)—as it was to their unmediated selves, and gives herself into the patriarchy toward which her defensive behavior all along has been in reference.

Yet in *As You Like It* a tissue of metadramatic discourse has been woven through and around this penultimate sublimation of the self-consciously fictive mode of romance to the redeemed biblical "realism" of its patrilinear plot that may help us suggest what "kind" of pastoral this play finally is. During the course of their comic wooing Audrey queries Touchstone, "I do not know what 'poetical' is. Is it honest in deed and word? Is it a true thing?" to which Touchstone replies, "No, truly; for the truest poetry is the most feigning, and lovers are given to poetry; and what they swear in poetry may be said as lovers they do feign" (3.3.17–22). Now Touchstone would dearly love to find Audrey a little more poetical, for then, despite her protestations, she might feign/fain (pretend/desire) to lie (to tell a falsehood/ to copulate), and either way he might get to have sex with her. But more seriously, his reply and the play's constant allusions to the analogous powers of poetry and sexual relations to make something like, but other than, the previously existing reality have relevance to the metadramatic question of what its action produces in us, its audience. Is poetry merely a lie, or does it work to give apprehensible form to our desires? And what, we ask as feminist critics, are these desires?

As You Like It is the ultimately contextual play. Despite its very firm grounding in contemporary social realities and the conventions of romantic and heroic discourse, the play remains conscious that its pastoral inside reflects a playful outside of continuing interpretation. Thus act 3, scene 2, the initial scene of pastoral negotiation, is prefaced by a debate between Touchstone and Corin on the significance of "this shepherd's life," in which the old shepherd's simple and appropriate tautologies are circumscribed by Touchstone's courtly wit. Touchstone does not decenter the mysterious *esse* of Arden, any more than he discomposes Corin, but he does remind us that as sophisticated, postlapsarian auditors we will never be content to rest here. Structured as a debate in all its details and its major patterns, *As You Like It* also invites us to enter its debates, ourselves "busy actor[s] in their play" (3.4.56).

On the specific issue of the play's treatment of gender identity and sex roles, we need finally to move beyond Rosalind's defensive fears, her complex interaction as Ganymede/Rosalind, and her resubmission of herself to the restored patriarchy of her noble father and tested lover to consider the altered environment of the last movement of the play, including Rosalind's invocation of magic, and the play's metadramatic "Epilogue."

For all its self-conscious artfulness, its impositions and nuances of style, a part of this play remains beyond man's control and is discovered in action. As the play closes, that part, suddenly, and without explanation, turns benign: "the icy fang / And churlish chiding of the winter's wind" (2.1.6–7) turns to "spring time, the only pretty [ring] time" (5.3.19); Rosalind/Ganymede's fictional misogynistic "old religious uncle" (3.2.343–50) becomes an equally fictional but now romantically helpful "magician, most profound in his art, and yet not damnable" (5.2.60–61; see also 5.4.30–34); and from beyond any rational expectations that the text has established, the god Hymen comes to "atone" the play, wedding earth and heaven, country and town. Hymen's own words can serve as an hermeneutic for this final movement of the play: "Feed yourselves with questioning; / That reason wonder may diminish" (5.4.138–39). Rational interpretation and the conversations that the characters conduct beneath Hymen's nuptial lyric can explain in great part how these characters have come together. But though "reason wonder may diminish," it cannot cancel it altogether.

The play has worked toward evoking an atmosphere of wonder and a promise of fresh beginnings that Touchstone's realism or Duke Frederick's and Jaques's contemplative withdrawals can anchor but not destroy. *As You Like It* transforms the problem of sexual relations insofar as it suggests a world of possibility for the continued negotiation of these differences.

In the metadramatic "Epilogue" the continued negotiation of sexual difference becomes the tentative metaphor for the most successful art. Here, for once, men bear the greater burden. The Elizabethan boy actor who played Rosalind conjures women to please themselves and men to play with women for mutual pleasure:

> My way is to conjure you, and I'll begin with the women. I charge you, O women, for the love you bear to men, to like as much of this play as please you; and I charge you, O men, for the love you bear to women (as I perceive by your simp'ring, none of you hates them), that between you and the women the play may please.
>
> ("Epilogue," 11–17)

He thus inverts the sexological situation of the play itself, where Orlando had but to become assured in his male heroic identity, while Rosalind had had, through her disguise, her "double-voiced" discourse, to accommodate herself to him. This final inversion in this consummately playful play suggests that men and women can work together—albeit often awkwardly—to transform a world not deterministically bound by its cultural conventions.

Much of Shakespeare's later career suggests how difficult that is. *As You Like It* itself delicately skirts, with the Duke's sweet style, Orlando's simple heroism, and Rosalind's self-restraint, the excoriating issue of the nonfeminist maternal subtext that will erupt in Shakespeare's tragedies. Although we may use Rosalind's double-voiced discourse and the final metadramatic openness of the play to decenter its patriarchal assumptions, Shakespeare's later plays gravitate around the threat to these values represented by a woman's projected infidelity, the "nothing" that is the source of her reproductive power. In closing I can only hazard some of the symptoms and causes of this shift from comic playfulness to tragic anxiety about sexuality.

I believe that as Shakespeare perfected his romantic comedies and the movement toward marriage within them, he was compelled to face more directly the threat *within* marriage that coincides with the metaphysical and political crisis uncovered in his history plays. If, as the history plays suggest, there is no clear divine sanction for ruling, nor any untainted or disinterested human succession, you confront your origin in the female body, where no one really knows his father: "there," as Othello cries, "where I have garner'd up my heart, / Where either I must live or bear no life; / The fountain from the which my current runs / Or else dries up" (Othello, 4.2.57–60). Literary conventions such as the traditional chaste inaccessibility of the idealized lady and the use of boy actors to play female parts might shield Shakespeare for a time from this threat of the female body, allowing him, in the romantic comedies, to experiment with a dazzling series of sexual permutations that we may now appropriate for our own ends. But Shakespeare also deconstructs these literary conventions in the course of his plays in a way that brings him up against the new social realities of marriage and the family in early modern Europe, where decline of external religious authority, loss of feudal power, urban centralization, and nascent capitalism all function to alienate actual women while making their sexuality the focus of ever more anxious regard. Within Shakespeare's career As You Like It offers us a brief moment of tremulous poise before we sound those depths.

Chronology

1564	William Shakespeare born at Stratford-on-Avon to John Shakespeare, a butcher, and Mary Arden. He is baptized on April 26.
1582	Marries Anne Hathaway in November.
1583	Daughter Susanna born, baptized on May 26.
1585	Twins Hamnet and Judith born, baptized on February 2.
1588–90	Sometime during these years, Shakespeare goes to London, without family. First plays performed in London.
1590–92	*The Comedy of Errors*, the three parts of *Henry VI*.
1593–94	Publication of *Venus and Adonis* and *The Rape of Lucrece*, both dedicated to the Earl of Southampton. Shakespeare becomes a sharer in the Lord Chamberlain's company of actors. *The Taming of the Shrew*, *The Two Gentlemen of Verona*, *Richard III*, *Titus Andronicus*.
1595–97	*Romeo and Juliet*, *Richard II*, *King John*, *A Midsummer Night's Dream*, *Love's Labor's Lost*.
1596	Son Hamnet dies. Grant of arms to Shakespeare's father.
1597	*The Merchant of Venice*, *Henry IV, Part 1*. Purchases New Place in Stratford.
1598–1600	*Henry IV, Part 2*, *As You Like It*, *Much Ado about Nothing*, *Twelfth Night*, *The Merry Wives of Windsor*, *Henry V*, and *Julius Caesar*. Moves his company to the new Globe Theatre.
1601	*Hamlet*. Shakespeare's father dies, buried on September 8.
1601–2	*Troilus and Cressida*.
1603	Death of Queen Elizabeth; James VI of Scotland becomes James I of England; Shakespeare's company becomes the King's Men.
1603-4	*All's Well That Ends Well*, *Measure for Measure*, *Othello*.

1605–6	*King Lear, Macbeth*.
1607	Marriage of daughter Susanna on June 5.
1607–8	*Timon of Athens, Antony and Cleopatra, Pericles, Coriolanus*.
1608	Shakespeare's mother dies, buried on September 9.
1609	*Cymbeline*, publication of sonnets. Shakespeare's company purchases Blackfriars Theatre.
1610–11	*The Winter's Tale, The Tempest*. Shakespeare retires to Stratford.
1612–13	*Henry VIII, The Two Noble Kinsmen*.
1616	Marriage of daughter Judith on February 10. Shakespeare dies at Stratford on April 23.
1623	Publication of the Folio edition of Shakespeare's plays.

Contributors

HAROLD BLOOM, Sterling Professor of the Humanities at Yale University, is the author of *The Anxiety of Influence, Poetry and Repression,* and many other volumes of literary criticism. His forthcoming study, *Freud: Transference and Authority,* attempts a full-scale reading of all of Freud's major writings. A MacArthur Prize Fellow, he is general editor of five series of literary criticism published by Chelsea House. During 1987-88, he served as Charles Eliot Norton Professor of Poetry at Harvard University.

C. L. BARBER was Professor of Literature at the University of California, Santa Cruz. His books include *Shakespeare's Festive Comedy.*

THOMAS MCFARLAND, Murray Professor of English at Princeton University, is the author of *Shakespeare's Pastoral Comedy, Tragic Meanings in Shakespeare, Coleridge and the Pantheist Tradition,* and *Romanticism and the Forms of Ruin.*

ROSALIE COLIE was Professor of English at Brown University until her death in 1972. She is the author of *Paradoxia Epidemica, The Resources of Kind, Shakespeare's Living Art,* and a book of poems, *Atlantic Wall and Other Poems.*

RUTH NEVO is Professor of English at Hebrew University in Jerusalem. She is the author of *The Dial of Virtue: A Study of Poems on Affairs of State in the Seventeenth Century, Comic Transformations in Shakespeare,* and *Tragic Form in Shakespeare.* She has also translated into English the *Selected Poems* of Chaim Nachman Bialik.

LOUIS ADRIAN MONTROSE is Professor of English Literature at the University of California at San Diego. He is the author of several articles on Elizabethan drama and poetry and is currently completing a book on the representation of Queen Elizabeth in Elizabethan Culture.

151

PETER ERICKSON teaches English at Wesleyan University and is the author of *Patriarchal Structures in Shakespeare's Drama*.

BARBARA J. BONO is Assistant Professor of English at the University of Michigan at Ann Arbor. She has written articles on Shakespeare and William Morris.

Bibliography

Allen, Michael J. B. "Jaques against the Seven Ages of the Proclan Man." *Modern Language Quarterly* 42, no. 4 (December 1981): 331–46.

Bamber, Linda. *Comic Women, Tragic Men: A Study of Gender and Genre in Shakespeare*. Stanford: Stanford University Press, 1982.

Barber, C. L. *Shakespeare's Festive Comedy*. Princeton: Princeton University Press, 1959.

Barton, Anne. *"As You Like It* and *Twelfth Night:* Shakespeare's Sense of an Ending." In *Shakespearean Comedy,* edited by Malcolm Bradbury and D. J. Palmer, 160–82. Stratford-upon-Avon Studies 14, 1972.

Bennett, Robert B. "The Reform of a Malcontent: Jaques and the Meaning of *As You Like It." Shakespeare Studies* 9 (1976): 188–98.

Berry, Edward I. "Rosalynde and Rosalind." *Shakespeare Quarterly* 31 (1980): 42–52.

———.*Shakespeare's Comic Rites.* Cambridge: Cambridge University Press, 1984.

Berry, Ralph. *Shakespeare's Comedies: Explorations in Form.* Princeton: Princeton University Press, 1972.

Bethell, S. L. *Shakespeare and the Popular Dramatic Tradition.* Durham, N.C.: Duke University Press, 1944.

Bracher, Mark. "Contrary Notions of Identity in *As You Like It." Studies in English Literature* 24, no. 2 (Spring 1984): 225–40.

Bristol, Michael D. *Carnival and Theater: Plebeian Culture and the Structure of Authority in Renaissance England.* New York and London: Methuen, 1985.

Carroll, William C. *The Metamorphoses of Shakespearean Comedy.* Princeton: Princeton University Press, 1985.

Daley, A. Stuart. "Where Are the Woods in *As You Like It?" Shakespeare Quarterly* 34, no. 2 (Summer 1983): 172–80.

Erickson, Peter B. *Patriarchal Structures in Shakespeare's Drama.* Berkeley and London: University of California Press, 1985.

Erickson, Peter B. and Kahn, Coppélia, eds. *Shakespeare's "Rough Magic": Renaissance Essays in Honor of C. L. Barber.* Newark: University of Delaware Press, 1985.

Frye, Northrop. *A Natural Perspective: The Development of Shakespearean Comedy and Romance.* New York: Columbia University Press, 1965.

Gardner, Helen. *"As You Like It."* In *More Talking of Shakespeare,* edited by John W. P. Garret, 17–32. London, Ayer Co., 1959.

Hale, John K. " 'We'll Strive to Please You Every Day': Pleasure and Meaning in Shakespeare's Mature Comedies." *Studies in English Literature* 21, no. 2 (Spring 1981): 241–55.

Hayles, Nancy K. "Sexual Disguise in *As You Like It* and *Twelfth Night.*" *Shakespeare Survey* 32 (1979): 63–72.

Kelly, Thomas. "Shakespeare's Romantic Heroes: Orlando Reconsidered." *Shakespeare Quarterly* 24 (Winter 1973): 22–32.

Knowles, Richard. "Myth and Type in *As You Like It.*" *ELH* 33 (1966): 1–22.

Leggatt, Alexander. *Shakespeare's Comedy of Love.* London: Methuen, 1974.

McCombie, Frank. "Medium and Message in *As You Like It* and *King Lear.*" *Shakespeare Survey* 33 (1980): 67–80.

MacCrary, W. Thomas. *Friends and Lovers: The Phenomenology of Desire in Shakespearean Comedy.* New York: Columbia University Press, 1985.

Newman, Karen. *Shakespeare's Rhetoric of Comic Character: Dramatic Convention in Classical and Renaissance Comedy.* New York and London: Methuen, 1985.

Scoufos, Alice-Lyle. "The *Paradiso Terrestre* and the Testing of Love in *As You Like It.*" *Shakespeare Survey* 14 (1981): 215–27.

Taylor, Don Ervin. " 'Try in Time in Despite of a Fall': Time and Occasion in *As You Like It.*" *Texas Studies in Language and Literature* 24, no. 2 (Summer 1982): 121–36.

Taylor, Michael. "*As You Like It*: The Penalty of Adam." *Critical Quarterly* 15 (Spring 1973): 68–80.

Traci, Philip. "*As You Like It*: Homosexuality in Shakespeare's Play." *College Language Association Journal* 25, no. 1 (September 1981): 91–105.

Van den Berg, Kent T. *Playhouse and Cosmos: Shakespearian Theater as Metaphor.* Newark: University of Delaware Press, 1984.

Waddington, Raymond B. "Moralizing the Spectacle: Dramatic Emblems in *As You Like It.*" *Shakespeare Quarterly* 33, no. 2 (Summer 1982): 155–63.

Whall, Helen M. "*As You Like It*: The Play of Analogy." *Huntington Library Quarterly* 47, no. 1 (Winter 1984): 33–46.

Wheeler, Richard. *Shakespeare's Development and the Problem Comedies: Turn and Counter-Turn.* Berkeley and Los Angeles: University of California Press, 1981.

Young, David. *The Heart's Forest: A Study of Shakespeare's Pastoral Plays.* New Haven: Yale University Press, 1976.

Acknowledgments

"The Alliance of Seriousness and Levity in *As You Like It*" by C. L. Barber from *Shakespeare's Festive Comedy: A Study of Dramatic Form and Its Relation to Social Custom* by C. L. Barber, © 1959 by Princeton University Press. Reprinted by permission of Princeton University Press.

"For Other Than for Dancing Measures: The Complications of *As You Like It*" by Thomas McFarland from *Shakespeare's Pastoral Comedy* by Thomas McFarland, © 1972 by the University of North Carolina Press. Reprinted by permission of the author and the University of North Carolina Press.

"Perspectives on Pastoral: Romance, Comic and Tragic" by Rosalie Colie from *Shakespeare's Living Art* by Rosalie Colie, © 1974 by Princeton University Press. Reprinted by permission of Princeton University Press.

"Existence in Arden" by Ruth Nevo from *Comic Transformations in Shakespeare* by Ruth Nevo, © 1980 by Ruth Nevo. Reprinted by permission of Methuen & Co.

" 'The Place of a Brother' in *As You Like It*: Social Process and Comic Form" by Louis Adrian Montrose from *Shakespeare Quarterly* 32, no. 1 (Spring 1981), © 1981 by the Folger Shakespeare Library. Reprinted by permission of the *Shakespeare Quarterly*, published by the Folger Shakespeare Library.

"Sexual Politics and Social Structure in *As You Like It*" by Peter Erickson from *Patriarchal Structures in Shakespeare's Drama* by Peter Erickson, © 1985 by the Regents of the University of California. Reprinted by permission of the University of California Press. This essay originally appeared in *The Massachusetts Review* 23, no. 1 (Spring 1982), © 1982 by the Massachusetts Review, Inc. Reprinted by permission.

"Mixed Gender, Mixed Genre in Shakespeare's *As You Like It*" by Barbara J. Bono from *Renaissance Genres: Essays on Theory, History, and Interpretation* (Harvard English Studies 14), edited by Barbara Kiefer Lewalski, © 1986 by the President and Fellows of Harvard College. Reprinted by permission of the Department of English of Harvard University.

155

Index